FORM NEXT
TO FORM
NEXT TO FORM

FOR HEMI

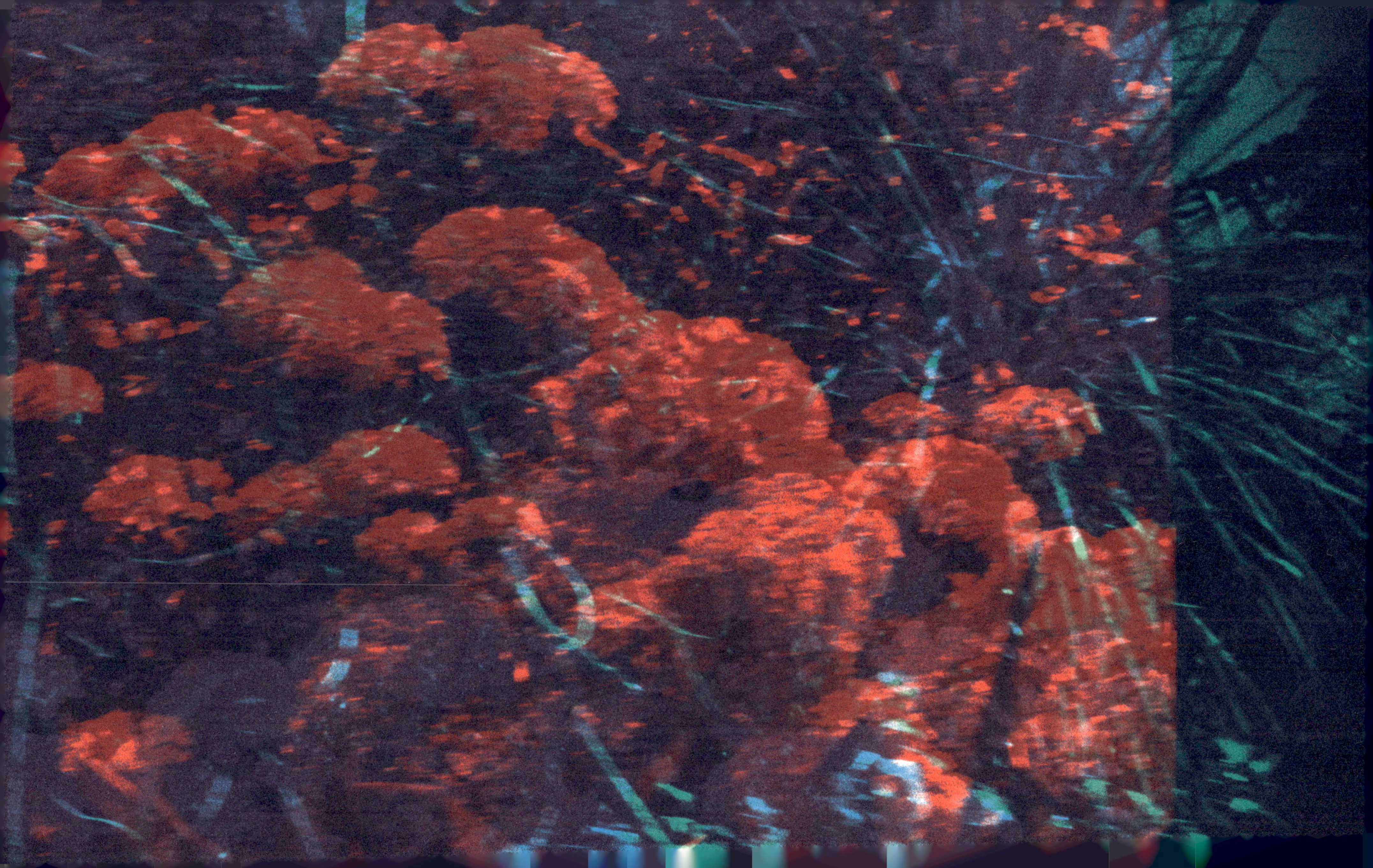

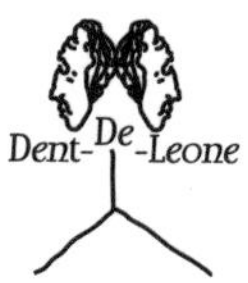

Dent-De-Leone

Clouds
PO Box 68187, Newton
Auckland 1145
Aotearoa New Zealand
Phone +64 9 309 2604
hello@clouds.co.nz
www.clouds.co.nz

ISBN: 978-0-9864628-7-0

Dent-De-Leone
48 Wilton Way
E8 1BG London
United Kingdom

info@dentdeleone.co.nz
www.dentdeleone.co.nz

ISBN: 978-1-907908-06-4

© 2012, Nova Paul, Clouds, Dent-De-Leone and contributors.

A catalogue record for this book is available from the National Library of New Zealand.

Editor: Gwynneth Porter
Designers: Åbäke
Printer: Die Keure, Belgium
Proofreader: Noel Porter
Clouds interns: Jack Hadley, Andrew Kennedy and Bryn Roberts

This publication was funded by Creative New Zealand Toi Aotearoa, and the School of Art and Design Research Fund, AUT University. The vinyl was funded by 1:12 Records.

Acknowledgements:
The artist would like to thank Nick Booth, Martino Gamper, Tessa Laird, Kim Martinengo, Dinah Paul, David Perry, Trish Scott, Kajsa Ståhl, Karl Steven, Maki Suzuki, Ben Tawhiti, Francis Upritchard, Katy Yiakmis, and WETAFX.

Form Next to Form Next to Form is a book made from stills from Nova Paul's 16mm film *This is not Dying* (2010). RGB print processes were used in its design to echo the RGB optical process of the three-colour-separation film itself. 'Whakarongo Mai,' played by Ben Tawhiti for *This is not Dying*, is reconfigured here on 7" LP.

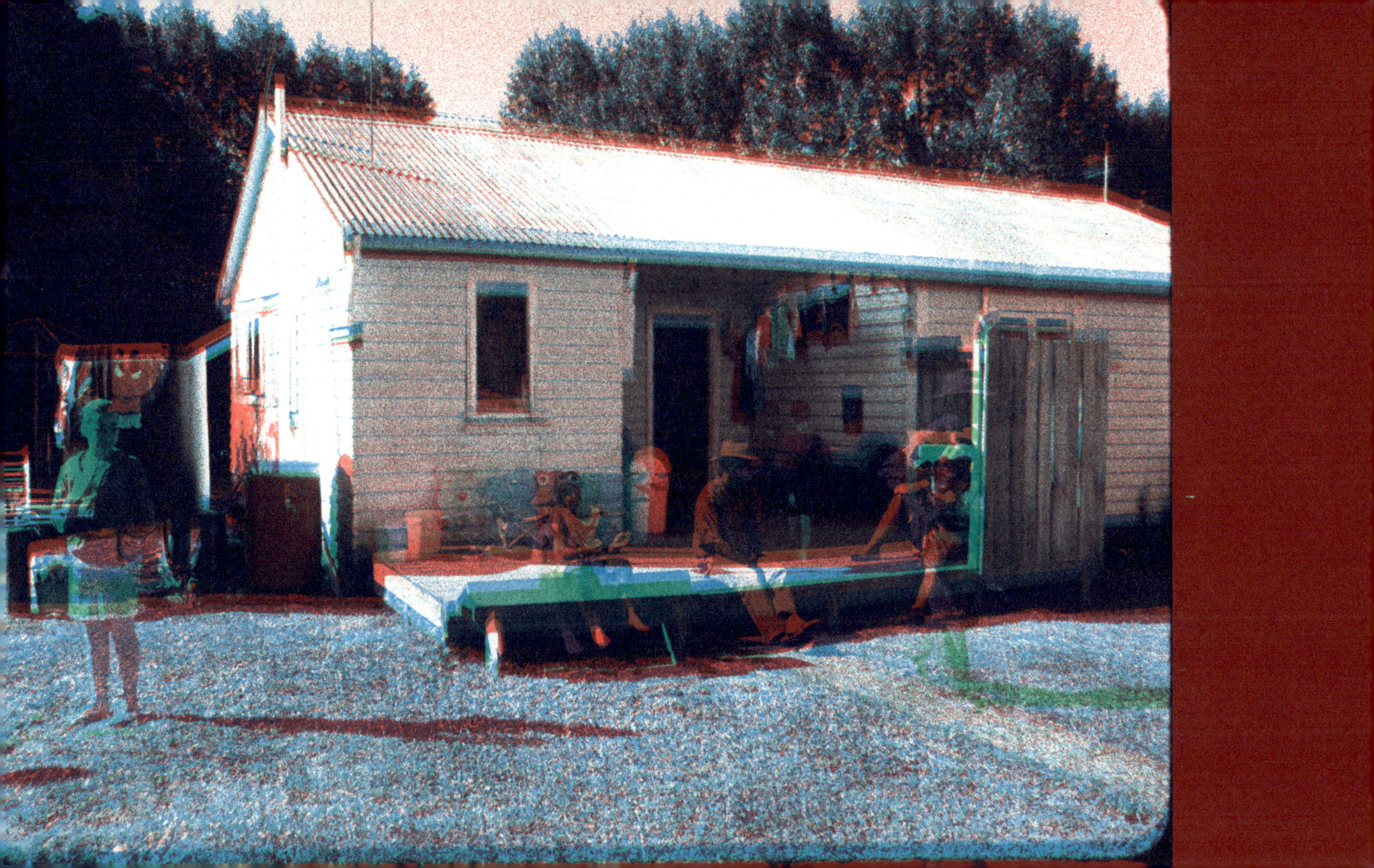

BEN TAWHITI

A musician for over 60 years, kaumatua Ben Tawhiti's career spans some of the most important developments in New Zealand music history, from the dance halls of the early post-war era through rock'n'roll and on to the 10:00 closing that many thought spelled the end of the golden age of professional musicianship in New Zealand.

Born and raised on Matakana Island in Tauranga harbour, Ben was surrounded by music from the first. His grandfather played for the celebrated Ratana Brass Band, and his uncles were all keen guitarists, gigging regularly around the region with their band The Beachcombers. These were pioneering days, and Ben's uncles would make their own steel guitars out of fence posts, carving them, installing the pick-ups from telephone receivers, and amplifying them using a Gulbransen radio lent by one of the island's elderly residents. Not yet in his teens, it was among The Beachcombers that Ben got his start as a performing musician during the 1940s, playing popular Hawaiian and Maori songs at dances from Whakatane to Paeroa and filling the halls of the day.

During and after college, Ben started stepping out with his own bands, emulating the success of his uncles' group and playing many of the same venues around the central North Island region. The musical capital of the country, however, was Auckland, and Ben soon relocated there. Upon his arrival, he was naturally attracted to the premier night-spot for musicians at the time, the Maori Community Centre in Freemans Bay. Ben would sit enthralled at the foot of the stage picking up tricks until eventually he was invited to play himself. With considerable experience under his belt already, and expertise in both lap steel and regular guitar, it was not long before Ben became a regular fixture at the community centre and a familiar face across the stages of the wider Auckland music scene.

Among Ben's many projects at this time was Benny's Five, a group that were one of the first wave of New Zealand rock acts to record and release locally penned songs rather than material written overseas. Arguably their most influential song, 'Haka Boogie' (the flip-side to 'Hawaiian Boogie') was also bilingual, featuring verses in Maori and choruses in both Maori and English. The song's centrepiece is Ben's impressive extended double solo, in which he struts his musical stuff to great effect, first on lap steel, then on 6-string electric.

In the early 1960s, at a time when many of his peers were trying their luck in Australia, America, and further afield, Ben, while invited to relocate overseas with the Maori Hi-Five, chose to remain in New Zealand with his young family. While he never relocated permanently, the mid-sixties did see Ben among an elite group of hotel and club musicians that played extensively through the Pacific Islands, including hotels in New Caledonia, Tahiti, and Fiji's celebrated Islay Club, memorable on account of being shaped like a giant Turtle Shell.

Back home in New Zealand, 1967 saw new liquor licensing laws allow pubs to stay open until 10:00pm, a change which, along with television, contributed to the demise of the large dance halls and the end of many dance bands. Pubs would sometimes book small combos to play, but as there was no dancing and the audience were seated, the show was restricted to the eyes and ears of the audience. It was around this time that Ben started the Ben Tawhiti Quartet, a group well skilled at tailoring their repertoire and delivery to the mood of the audience and adept at putting on a show for the eyes as much as the ears.

Their shows featured fancy synchronised footwork, instrument swapping, and displays of virtuosity such as playing their instruments behind their backs. The recipe was a success and the quartet enjoyed an incredible seven and a half year residency at the Milford Marina, playing six nights a week and spending their one 'day off' a week working up new material. Once again, Ben's craft, his choice of great collaborators, and his attention to the needs of the audience steered him safely through the shifting sands of the professional music scene.

For 'This is not Dying' Ben chose to play the traditional Nga Puhi ballad 'Whakarongo Mai' in response to Nova's iwi and the film's location. The film was played down in four passes as Ben recorded first rhythm, then lead, and then lead harmony on his 1952 Gibson Les Paul and then overdubbed a lap steel part on the guitar bought for him by his aunty upon his departure for New Caledonia in the mid-1960s. These takes were recorded through multiple amplifiers using close and room microphones to create 8 tracks of audio to accompany the film. Care was taken in the mix so that each of the 8 layers could respond to the pictures both in terms of the film's narrative, and with respect to the textures, colours, and other subtle visual elements present in the film.

— Karl Steven

THE VIRTUES OF TREES

Nova Paul and Gwynneth Porter

We head out into a paddock fringed with Puriri and Rewarewa forest, trees bearing names of ancestors — Te Arini, Te Pie, Te Mamae, Te Ruma — to bury the placenta of baby Hemi. After we finish the task we sit, resting in the shade of a giant Puriri tree that has large orchids growing in it. Dinah tells us that the early colonists called these widow-makers, as sometimes the weight of the plant causes them to fall on people passing beneath, especially after rain. She also said that the orchids have an intoxicating fragrance with a strong aphrodisiac power, particularly affecting men, and that many babies are born nine months after it flowers in September. The complex effect of sitting in the tree's etheric circuit was deeply relaxing, as if what I had previously thought was important had been pulled out of my nose as the ancient Egyptians removed the brains of the recently dead. There is a photograph of us all sitting under the Puriri tree, none of us aware that a photo was being taken. We are all off in different drifts, transported, daydreaming, who-knows-what is happening to us psychically. Rebooting most likely.

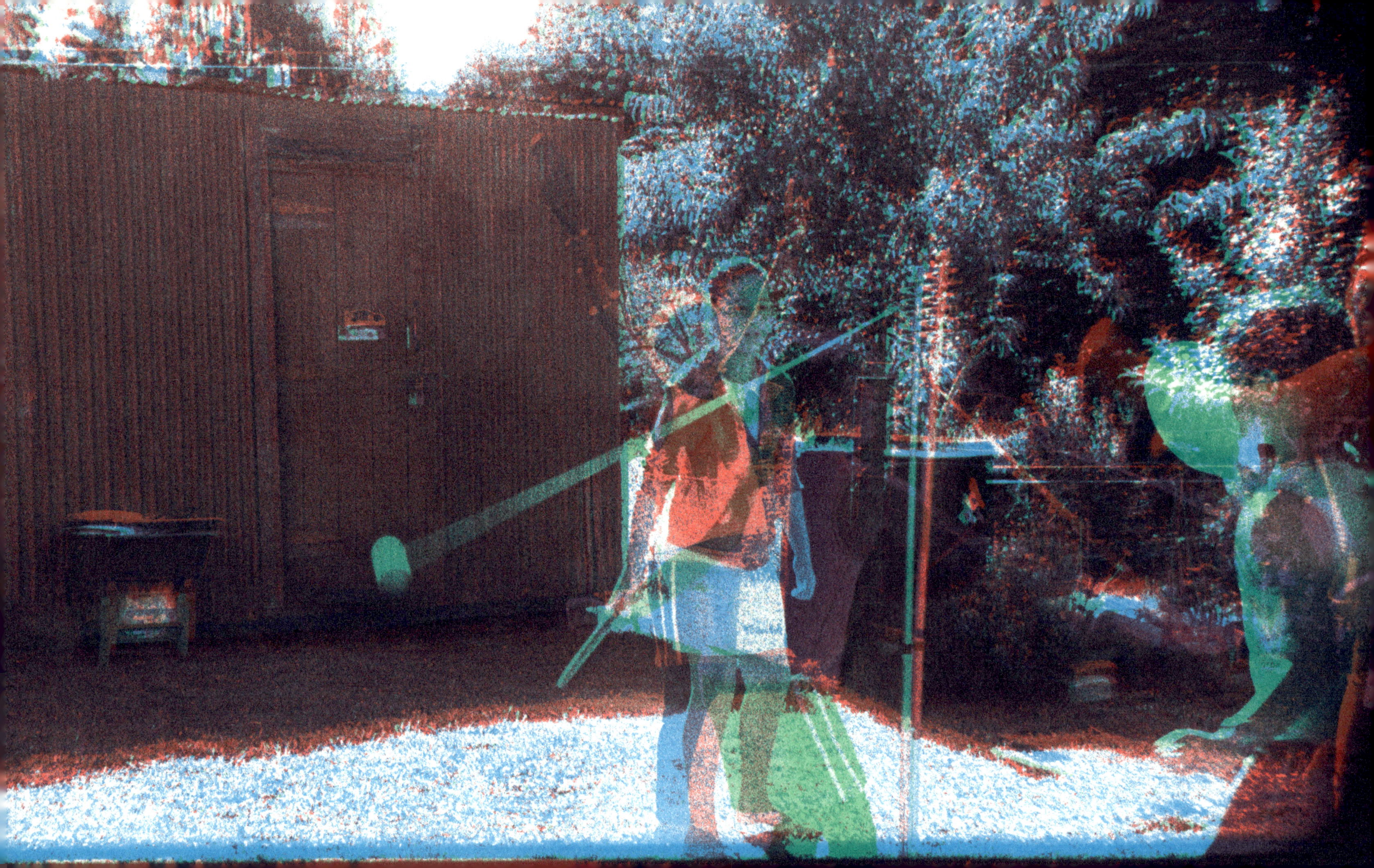

Time here has a different texture, more embodied than measured, and because of this there is a sense of freedom and ecstasy in being present. I've read that "ecstasy cannot be described other than by those who feel it, and I must go begging to those lucky ones. Nor does ecstasy have an internal order: the accumulation of sensations is therefore the only description."[1] Nova Paul's film *This is not Dying* (2010) captures simple moments from everyday activities carried out in the filmmaker's rural Maori family home and surrounding community. Filmed using the three-colour separation process, each sequence is made up of three shots — red, green and blue — that are composed later to form a single image with the entities of turquoise, pink, lilac, apricot mixing into a palette of purple, lemon, crimson. Figures cross each other's paths within the frame, blending with the environment and each other, constantly changing hue, register and form. It is as though they are channeling the animating force of light and the life of our psychic interior in the same stroke.

1. Antoni Negri, *Time for Revolution*, London and New York: Continuum, 2005, p.47.

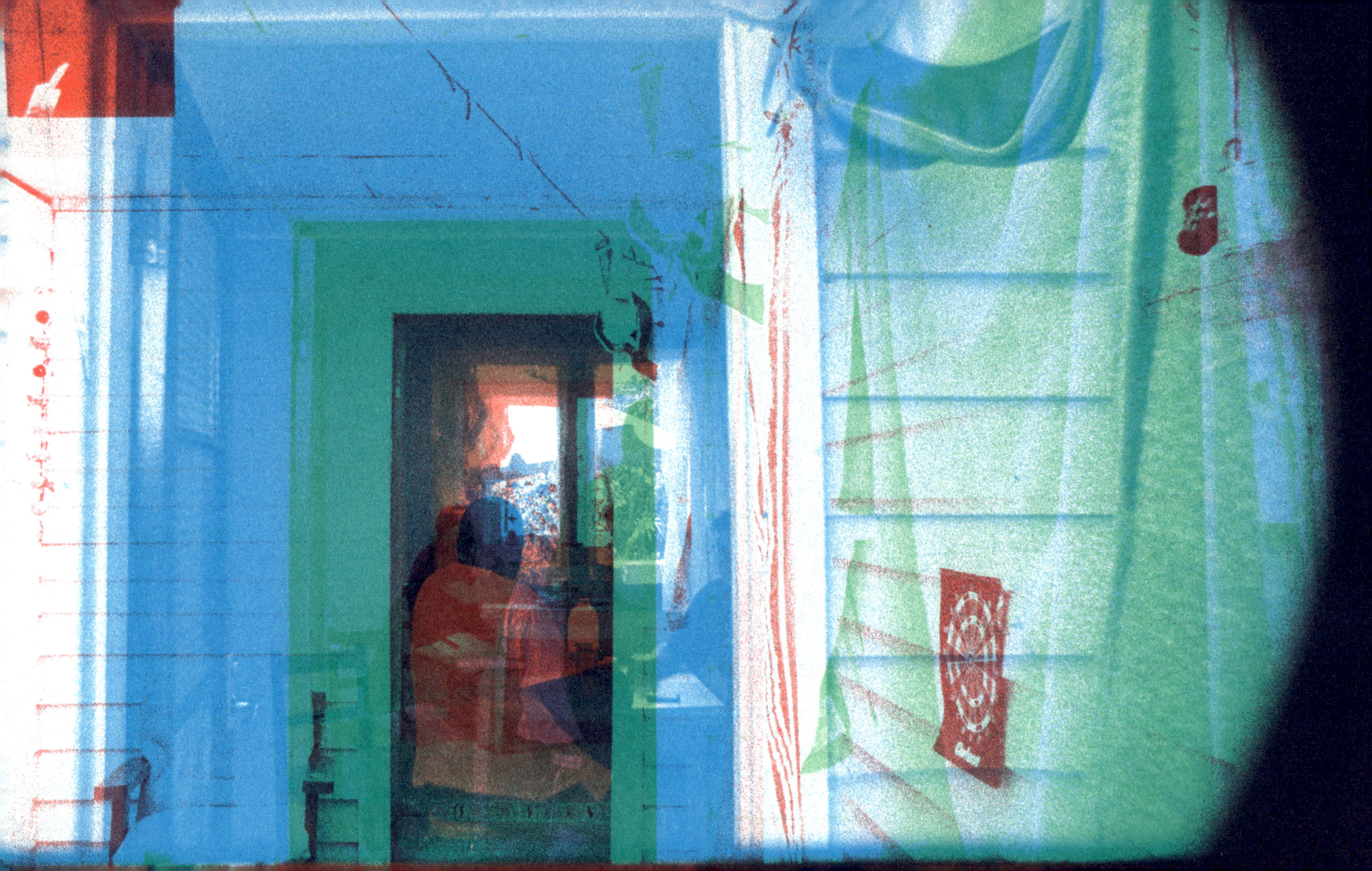

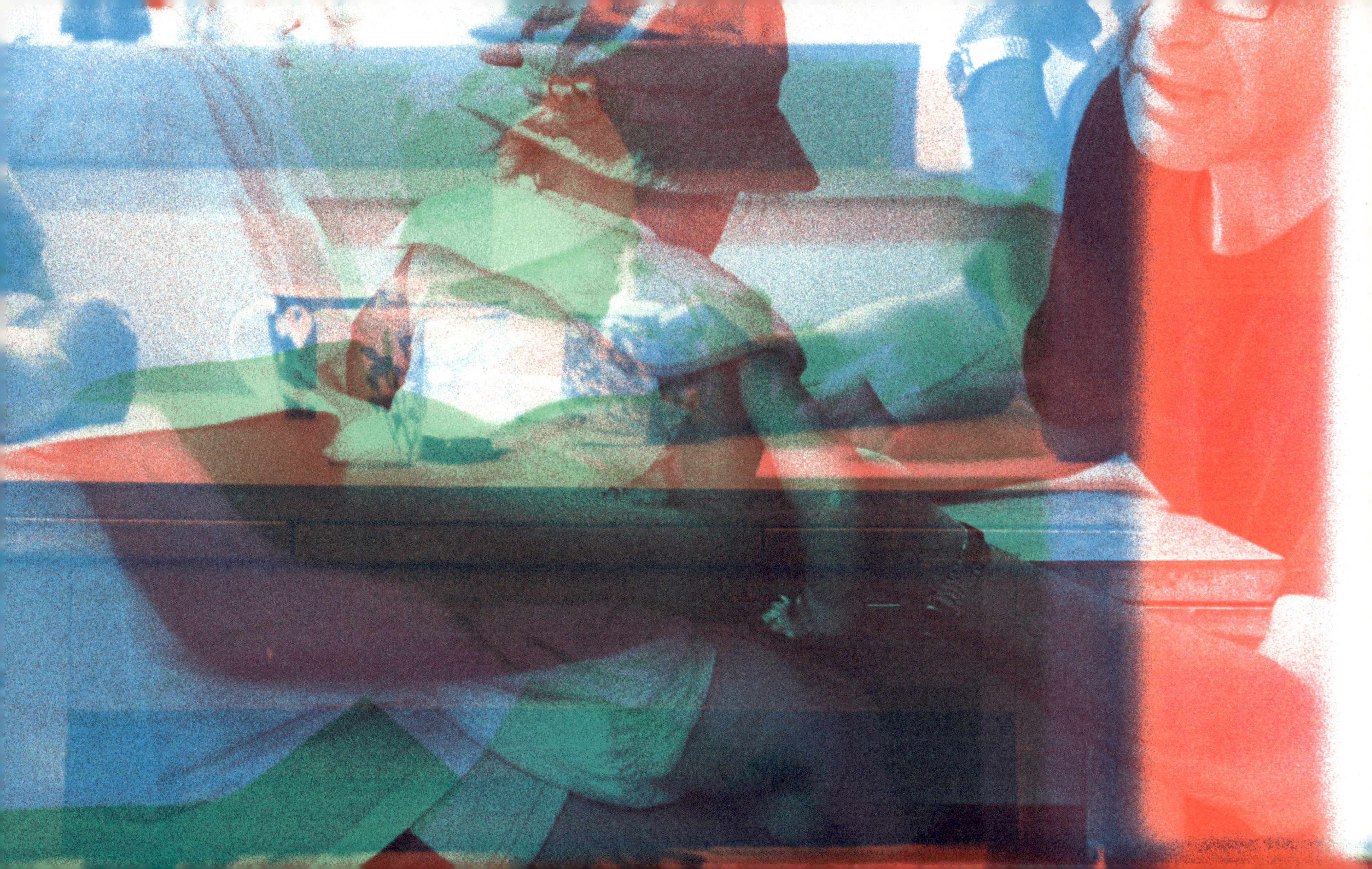

Visually, the film is made up of rays of light and coloured blocks. The shadows and interplay of smudged forms have the look of early 20th century abstract painting, with a similar effect — solid shapes dissolve and interrupt a standard filmic sense of being, time and place. And like the cubist artists who invented camouflage (to make the war disappear, thought the poet Jean Paulhan), parts of film are lost and hidden within surfaces that turn into a series of facets, while another sense of time is revealed and opened up. The kind of time that goes with deep reflection, stillness, sitting close to one another, that is not tethered to the usual flows of ordered time. The film's bleached and saturated palette, like the burning afterglow of an image behind closed eyelids, shares something intensely alive (proliferating, ebullient, liberated, transformative of sense and matter) and exciting with the methods of the Rayonists. As Larionov and Goncharova wrote in their 1913 manifesto:

"We perceive a sum of rays proceeding from a source of light… Now, if we concern ourselves not with the objects themselves but with the sums of rays from them, we can build a picture in the following way: The sum of rays from object A intersects the sum of rays from object B; in the space between them a certain form appears, and this is isolated by the artist's will… Perception, not of the object itself, but of the sum of rays from it, is, by its very nature, much closer to the symbolic surface of the picture than is the object itself. This is almost the same as the mirage which appears in the scorching air of the desert and depicts distant towns, lakes, and oases in the sky (in concrete instances)." Rayonism erases the barriers that exist between the picture's surface and nature. In *This is not Dying* planes filmed in three different takes collapse into intersecting planes of blazed light rebuilding a floating world, one where ancestors walk about with the living and the living connect with the place, a pure light within guiding their way on.

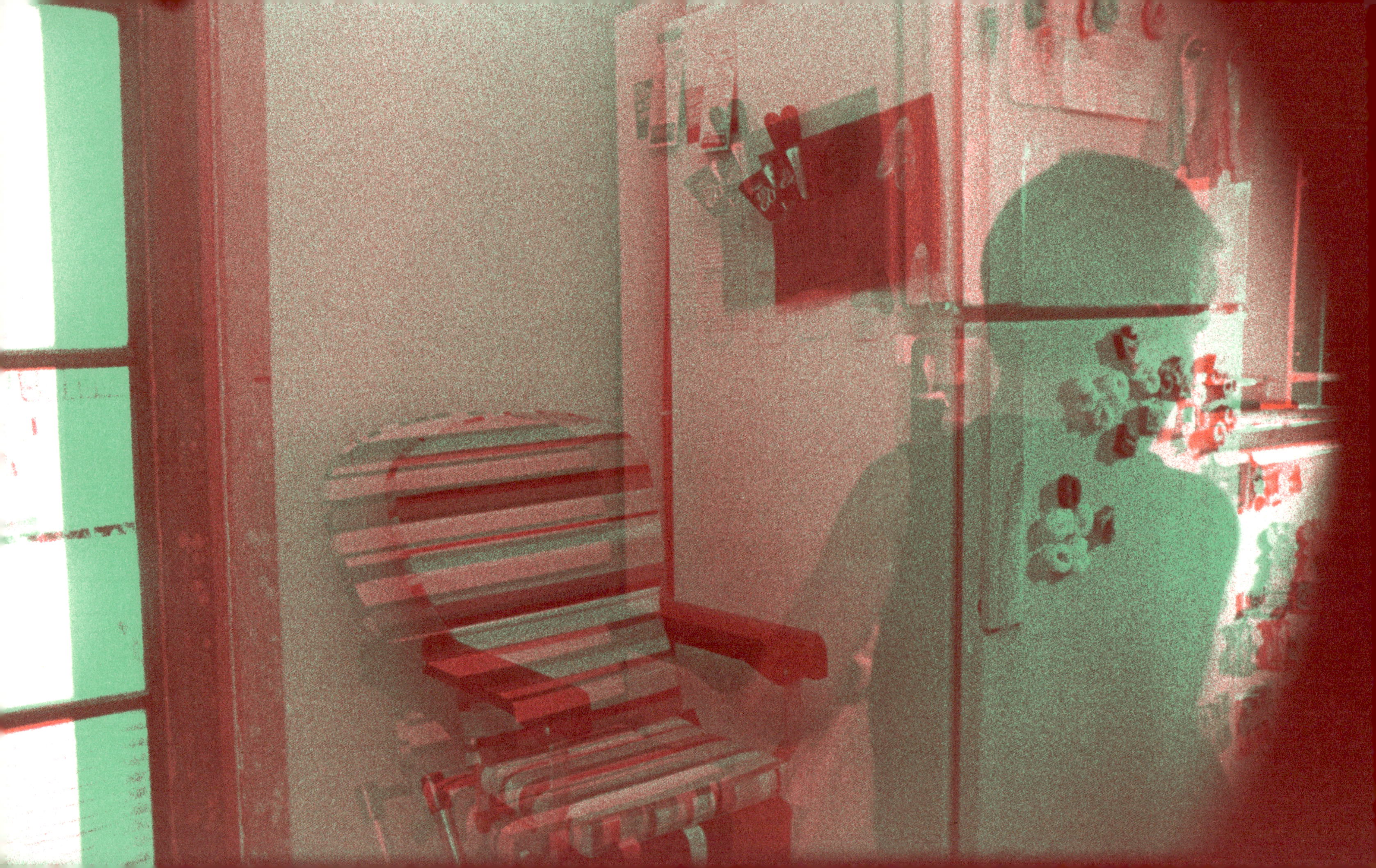

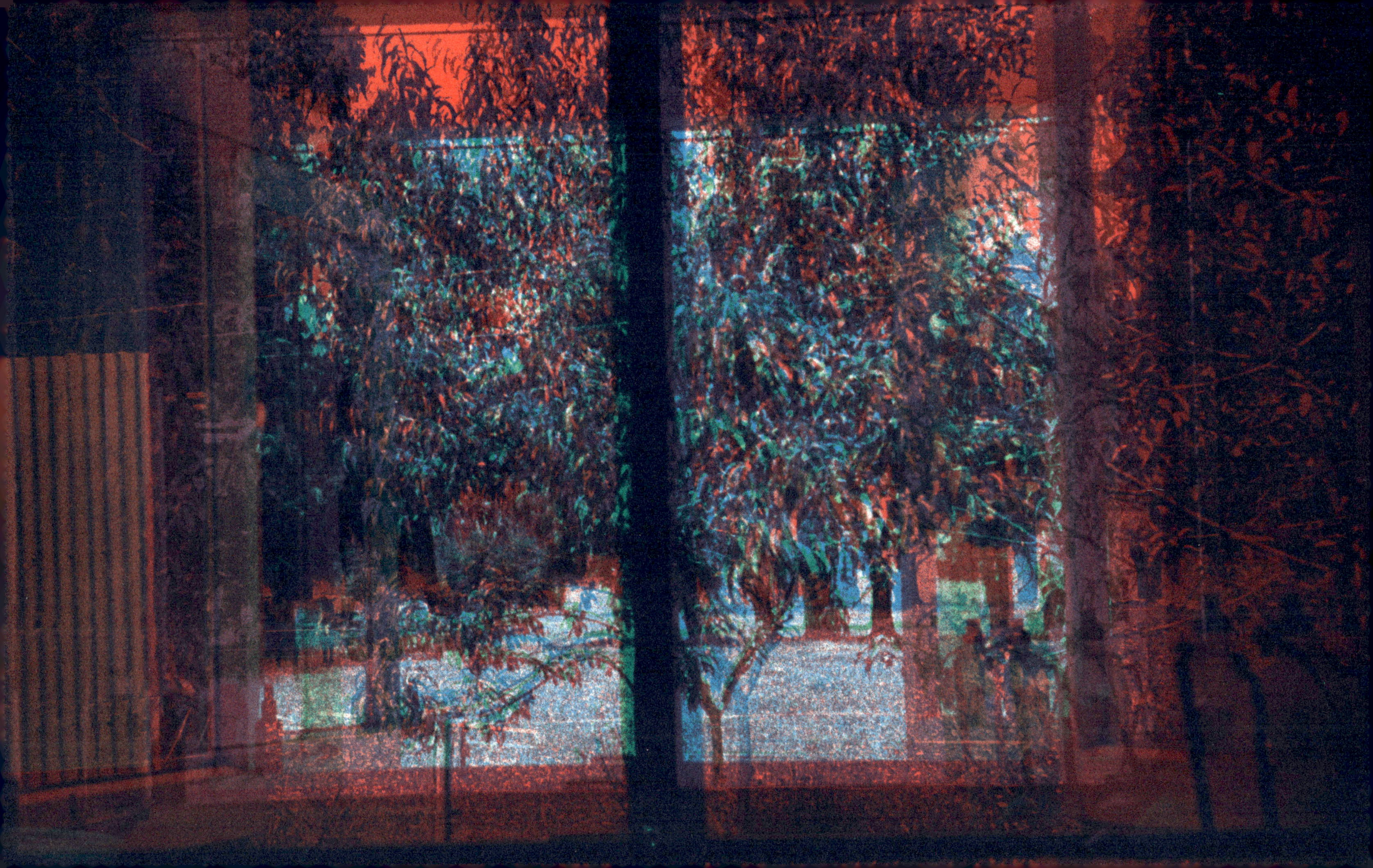

North of Auckland, under Whatitiri mountain, is a place that is little more than a group of houses but has long been the home of a Maori family. Early in the night, we show *This is not Dying* in the house that is central to the film, the small children under blankets on the couch and the grownups perched on kitchen chairs nodding a little in the dim light. They see their home and themselves through the light that is captured and bounced off their day-to-day activities like fixing motorbikes, preparing food for a communal meal at the marae, making tea in the kitchen, walking to the water-hole and bathing there. All is held together in the landscape, the landscape that holds and has held these people together for centuries. One of the children says sleepily of the people registered in the film that they look like ghosts but they aren't scary. This film feels like it has arisen out of a support structure, a place where the self can safely reconfigure in the company of others. There is a different, healing sense of time, a different "technology of the self"[2] for changing ourselves in the ways in which we discover we are open to grow, for our desires are holy.

2. See Michel Foucault, "Technologies of the Self" in L.H. Martin, H. Gutman and P.H. Hutton (eds) *Technologies of the Self: A Seminar with Michel Foucault*, Amherst: University of Massachusetts Press, 1988.

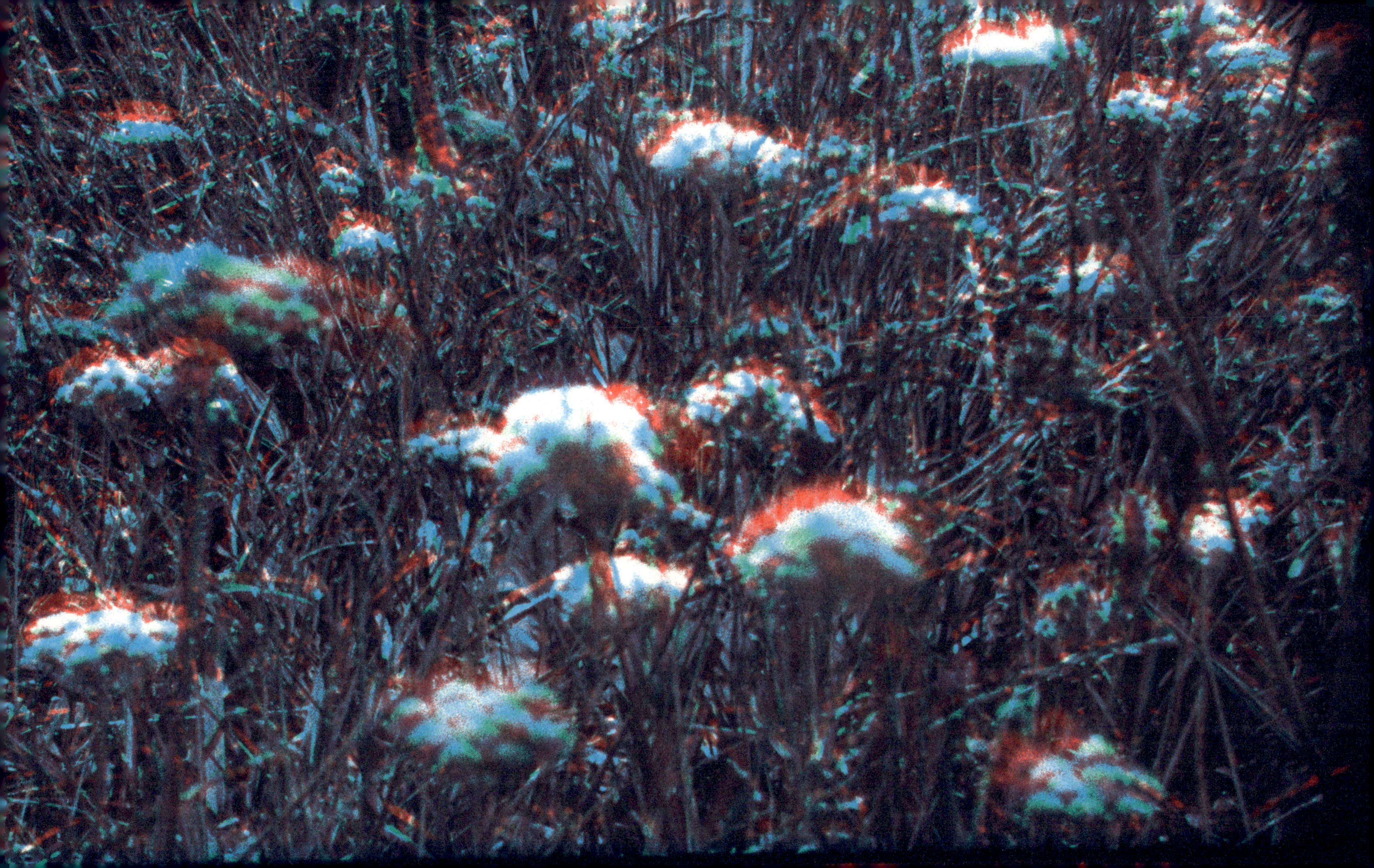

The time of this film is resistant to that ordering and levelling of souls experienced in the world of wage-labour. As the time-of-life of the worker is eroded by the demands of the workplace, and by the habits with which responsibility and precariousness are dealt with, the results are that the simple perception and connection with the present, and others, is seriously disturbed. Sociologist and political philosopher Antoni Negri describes this dominance of measured time over embodied time as creating emphasis on doing rather than being. When measured time takes over, "complexity is reduced to articulation,"[3] and singular meanings are promoted rather than experience being felt in full with its myriad of changing significances. Negri went on to say that "From another perspective, time can be entrusted to aesthetics, to genius, to recklessness, to music"[4], and this encourages me to think that the goal is to reclaim our time of life and basic creativity from the way it has been put to work.

3. Negri, p.47.
4. Ibid., p.48.

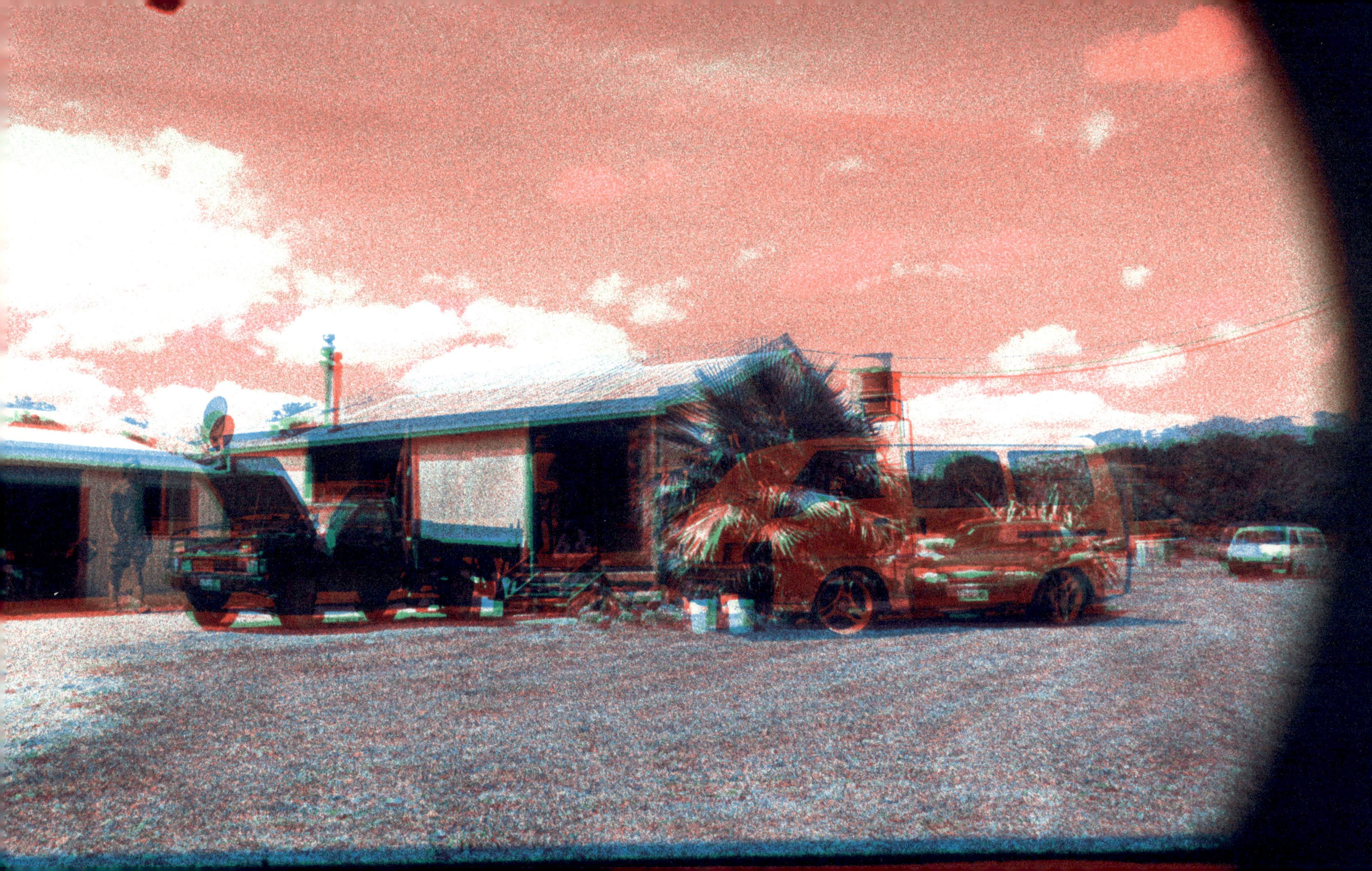

There's a searching in this film, not just for how to create the self, but what to aim for. What sorts of films make spaces, or act as support structures for the self-determination for the filmmaker and viewer both? Gardens are propagated with cuttings. Messages intended to be sent to the unconscious are always delivered, that is one idea. Another is that all language comes from trees. These stories overlap within us, collected and built together. When we trip we sense a shared becoming, immanence. We are present to the moment and attend to it collectively. This insight has been helpful for understanding how we work together, merge and make sense of the past by where we are now. It (affect) brings you into contact with the moment and creates a sense of touch. Up and down the river we go. Life always goes at several rhythms and at several speeds. I draw a line that leads up the stream from a grid of farmland blocks, onto the hillsides, inland towards the Hikurangi wetlands, to where my river Wairua starts. "As individuals and groups we are made of lines which are very diverse in nature – we have as many entangled lines as a hand. What we call with different names — schizoanalysis, micro-politics, pragmatics, diagrammatics, rhizomatics, cartography — is nothing else but the result of the study of the lines that we are."[5]

5. Gilles Deleuze and Claire Parnet, *Dialogues*, Paris: Flammarion, 1996, p.151.

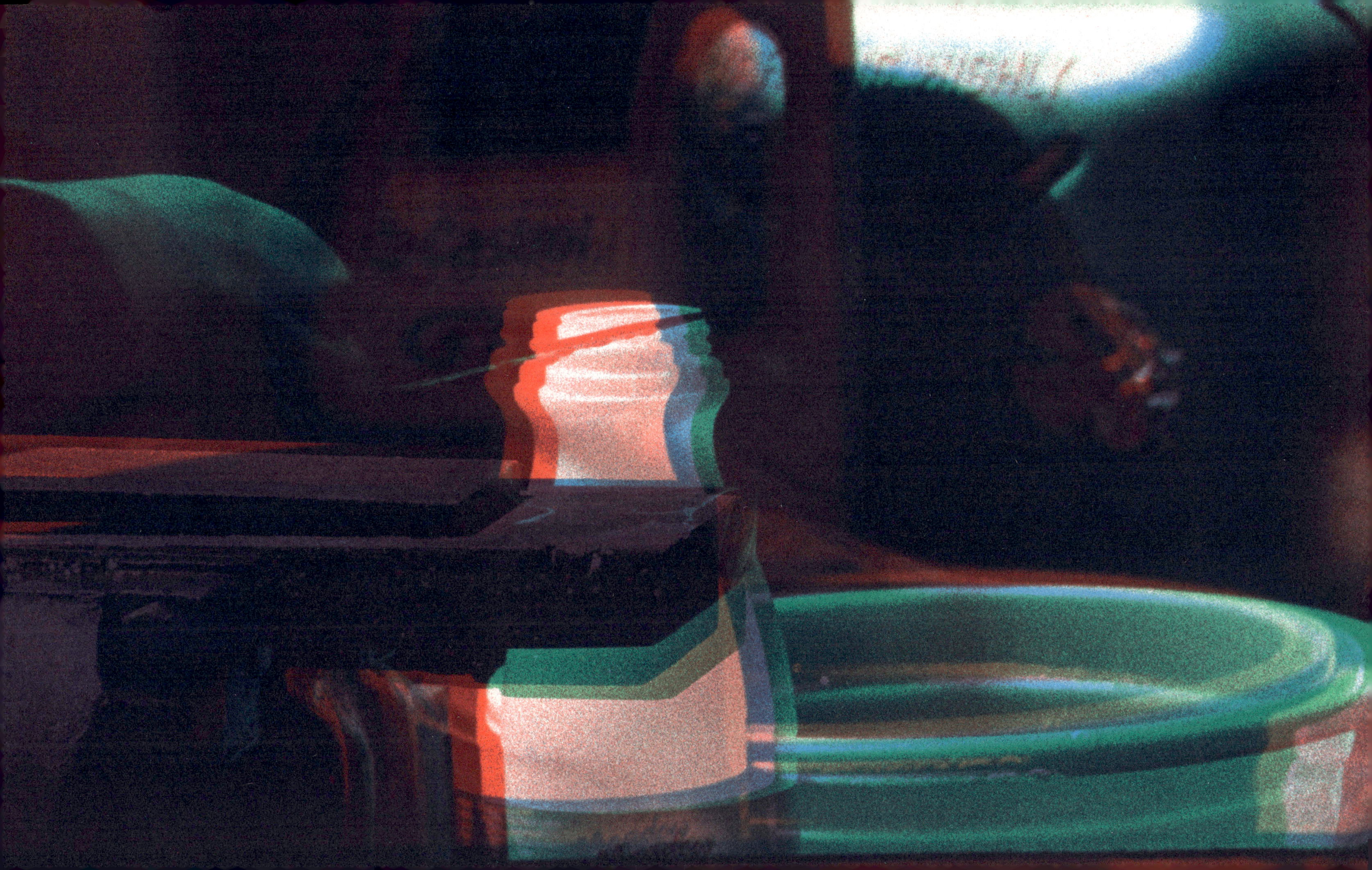

Contact with cold water makes our chakras spin, an esoteric elderly lady-neighbour tells me, reminding me that the full moon is the time for casting spells, and to make haste if I want anything to shift with the moon's energy this month. She was the one who told me that the Datura tree that had been growing by my door had died because it had taken something terrible from me that I had been holding on my own. She was also the one who gave me a South African 'sage' to smudge my house with, the smoke of which pulled me into a waking dream where I could smell flowers in the house. I later found out it was a dissociative hallucinogenic that is used to contact one's ancestors, and that smelling flowers or ripe fruit is the sign of a ghost visiting. I also learned that the limbic system of the brain that grows as we are loved is responsible for aspects of our emotions, behaviour, long-term memory and smell. I imagine it sitting on the back of our instinctual primitive lizard brain and knowing that because we are the latest physical embodiment of ancient genetic material, it is our job to act here because spirits can't.

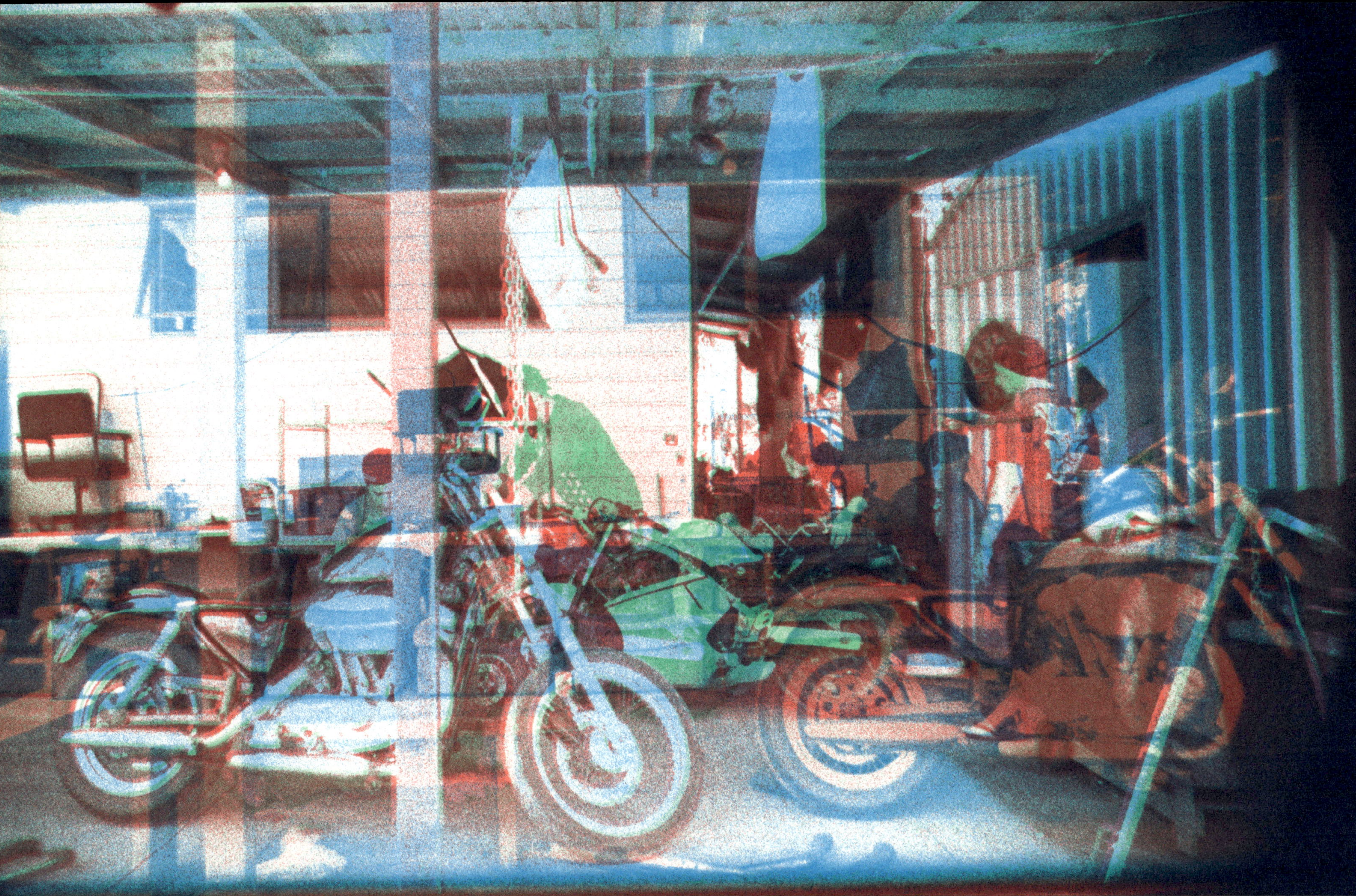

We're looking at a shrub with blotches of flowers, some white, some lilac, some dark purple. It's called Yesterday, Today and Tomorrow, and I wonder which flowers come first, light or dark? It's a plant that reminds us how to hold three moments, the past the present and future, in one form, in this moment. It is an act of balancing that takes lifetimes to achieve, and is borne of a willingness to allow a being there to take root above and below, without fear, haste, reservation, grasping or self-obsession. Quite an undertaking, and it won't pay. Yes, much of what has been created around this film was through sharing, talking, eating, walking around — all this takes time, time that sits outside the usual 'production time-lines' of film making. Barry Barclay writes of this as a way to capture the essence of the subject, where much is about listening and letting the environment figure itself, and for people to show themselves to each other in their own time and with cyclic methods of communication intact:

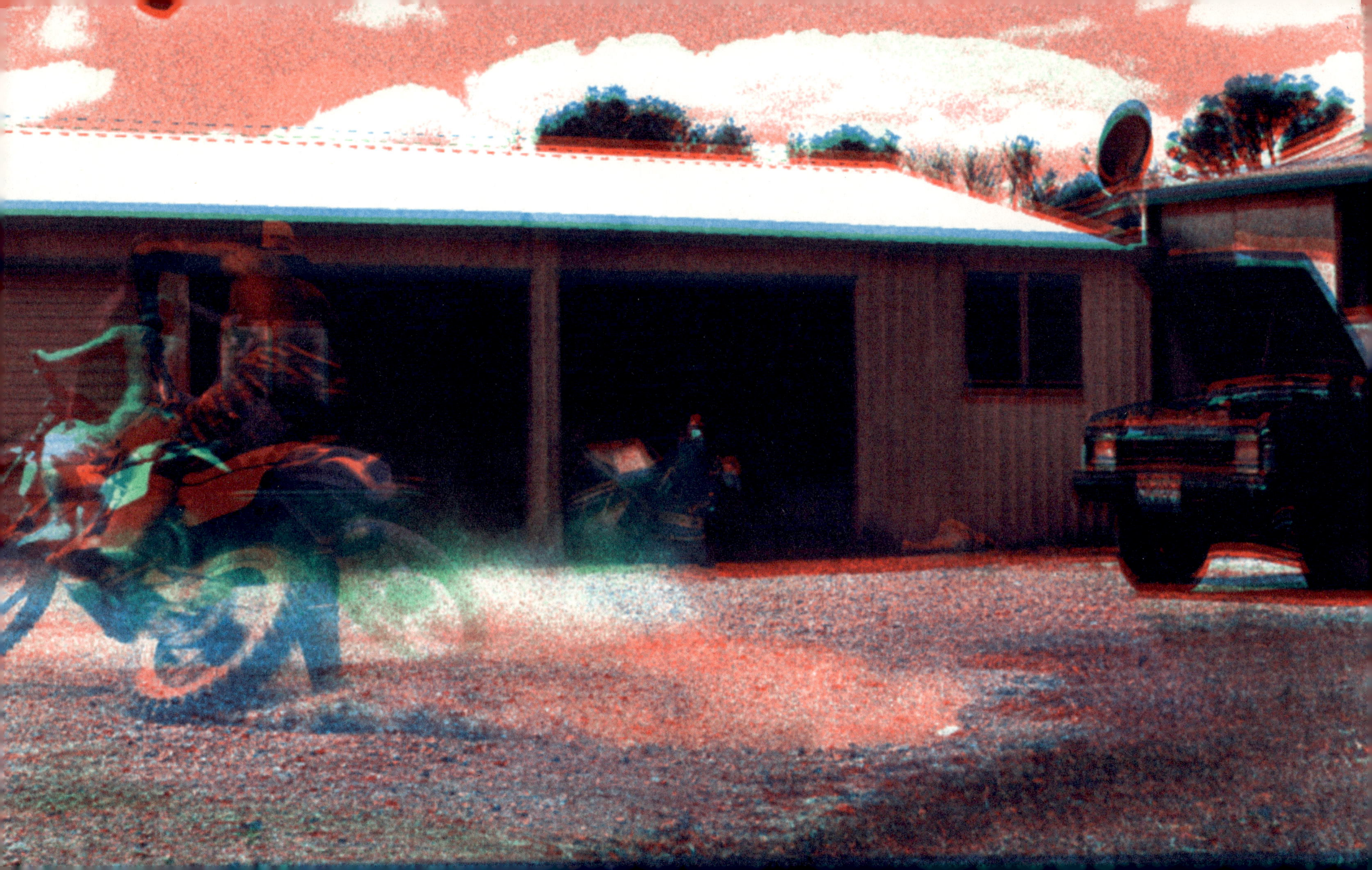

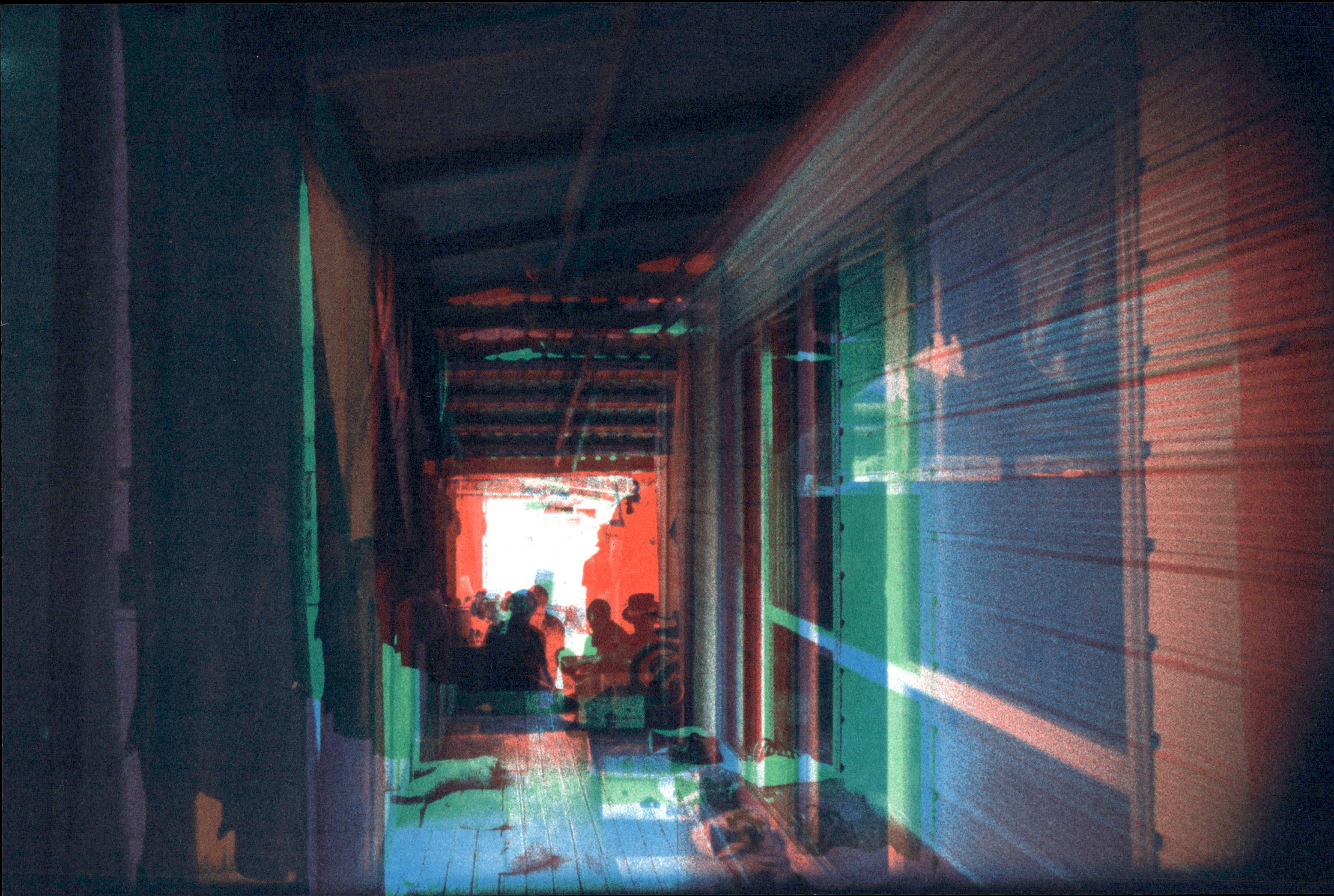

"To be any sort of Maori, you have to be a listener. You do not interrupt a person who is talking, no matter how humble that person may be — the rules about this are quite firm when formal talk is in progress. But a similar spirit is maintained even at informal occasions, such as a meal among relations, or chatting over a beer in a hotel. (…) One of the great glories of Maori life is that love of contact through talk. People will drive the length of the country to be present at a hui. There will be some important issue at stake probably, but between the formal discussions there will be time to sit on the steps of the meeting house, absorbing the conversations and contributing to them. People do not 'feel lost' on these occasions, but neither do they know 'exactly where they are going'. (…) I believe we might do well to further explore how to make the camera a listener. As a Maori, you are taught to be a listener; you sit at the feet and open your ears. You have no 'right to know'. The knowledge is gifted to you at appropriate times and in appropriate places. Those who do not have the patience and the humility to undergo this way of learning are unlikely to ever gain much of real depth."[6]

6. Barry Barclay, *Our Own Image*, Auckland: Longman Paul, 2000, pp.14–18.

In this film there is a sense of moving beyond the image, to a place where collective and individual stories, daydreams and unuttered wishes mingle. Agamben's assertion that gesture is the quality that underpins cinema rings true: "Cinema leads images back to the homeland of gesture, and so opening the sphere of ethos, the realm of ethics and politics. *Here nothing is being produced or acted, but rather something is being endured and supported*, becoming, a trying to figure something out that could not be sustained or articulated in language, it is being in the language of human beings."[7] As movement is caught in one of the filtered colours, sense and material build up as aggregations, like sedimentary geological forms, an accretion of layers. The first three-colour separation film Paul made, also without narration, was called *The Pink and White Terraces*, the title referring as much to a submerged geological wonder as to the filmmaking process of layering each take, each passage in time, to build up the image and to make a whole. Films in this body of work — there are now four — (in the philosopher Jacques Rancière's words) "abolish the opposition between the physical world of movement and the psychological world of the image."[8] As such they offer a resistance on the level of form to the terrible sameness brought down on our material and viewing culture.

7. Giorgio Agamben, *Means Without Ends: Notes on Politics*, Minneapolis: University of Minnesota Press, 2000.

8. Jacques Rancière, *Film Fables*, Oxford and New York: Berg, 2006, p.109.

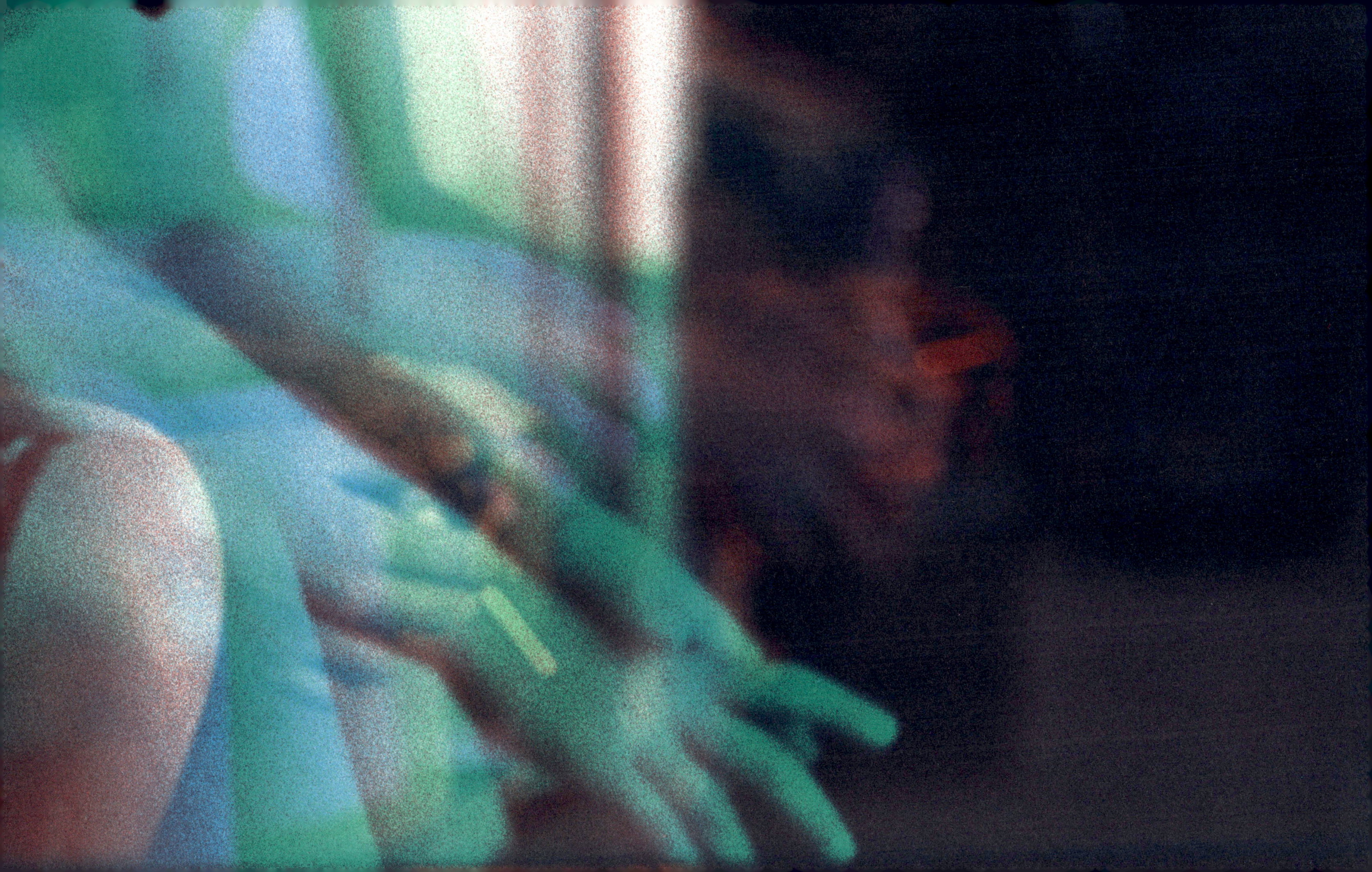

The music for the film *This is not Dying* is a folk song, a Nga Puhi love song, 'Whakaromo mai', and it starts as a karanga — a calling into the film, into a house and a homeland. Kaumatua Ben Tawhiti improvised this ballad on his steel and slide guitar, playing along with the images, using the men standing on the porch as the place to start, an anchor. It has a soundtrack but no dialogue to fix any thoughts — there in front of us is the ecstasy of being immersed in a visual experience, and how we may reflect on it, together. This is an existence. When we do not project into the future, even towards an honourable goal (the scourge of the good thing) and work with what and who is present and available to us (taking what is not ours is stealing), we allow experience to build up, like stairs. When I first heard the soundtrack, I thought of Gerry Garcia's improvised piece 'Love Song' for the acid scene in Michelangelo Antonioni's *Zabriskie Point* (1970). For this, away from The Grateful Dead and composed songs, he played along to footage of this legion of naked lovers in a film-company screening-cinema. His and Tawhiti's music has the same emergent quality, the same lilting tenderness, that falls apart and pulls together, drifts and fades — gaps caused by the pleasure of listening — and open sense of time and joy, in response to the tripped-out visuals. As Alphonso Lingis puts it "Outbursts of joy are visionary."[9] Both films' soundtracks are also rooted into folk traditions, in everyday experiences, in ordinary languages, the tactical speech of those who must work with givens[10].

9. Alphonso Lingis, *The First Person Singular*, Evanston: Northwestern University Press, 2007, p.49.

10. See Michel de Certeau, *The Practice of Everyday Life*, Berkeley: University of California Press, 1984.

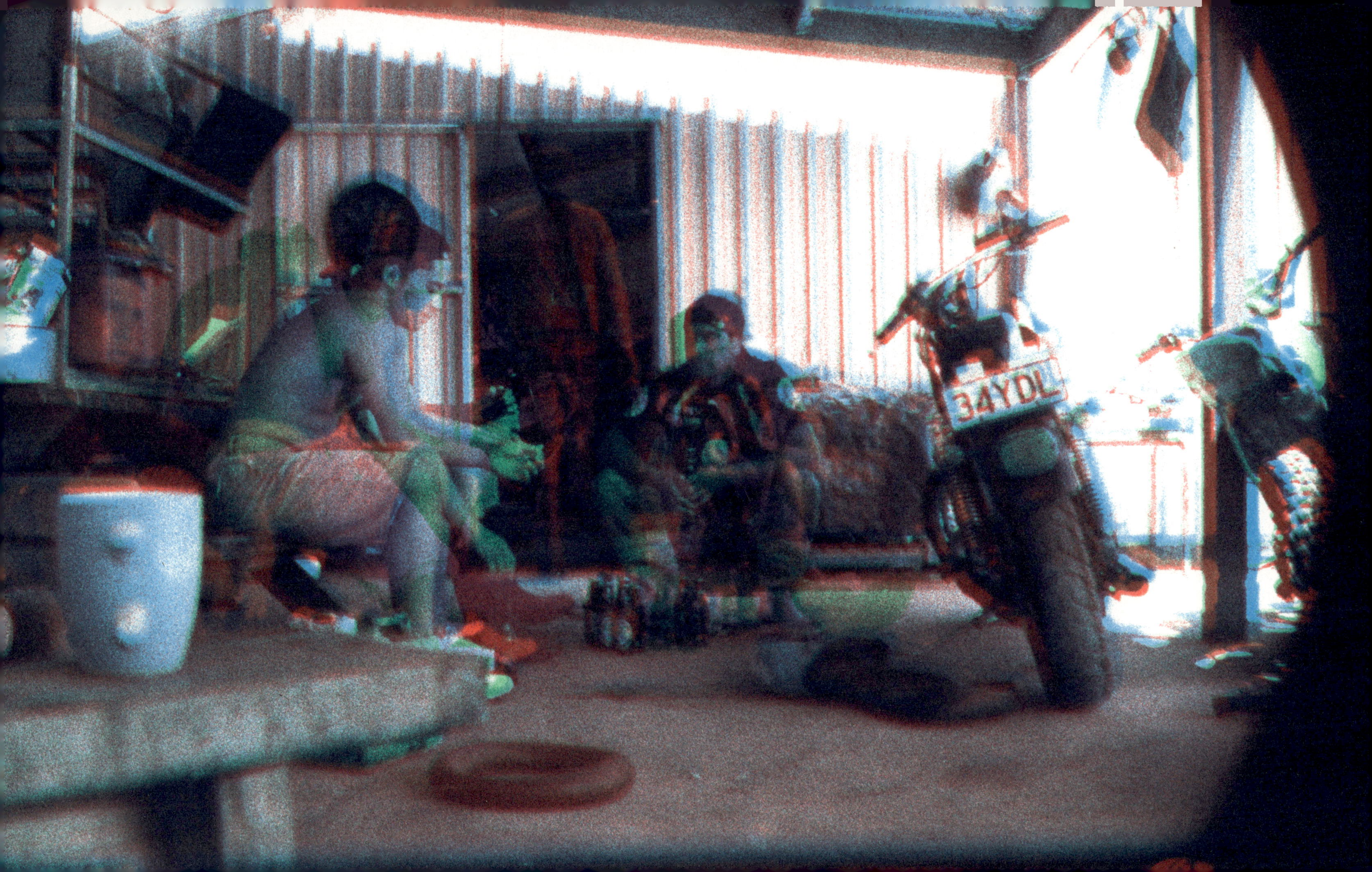
34YDL

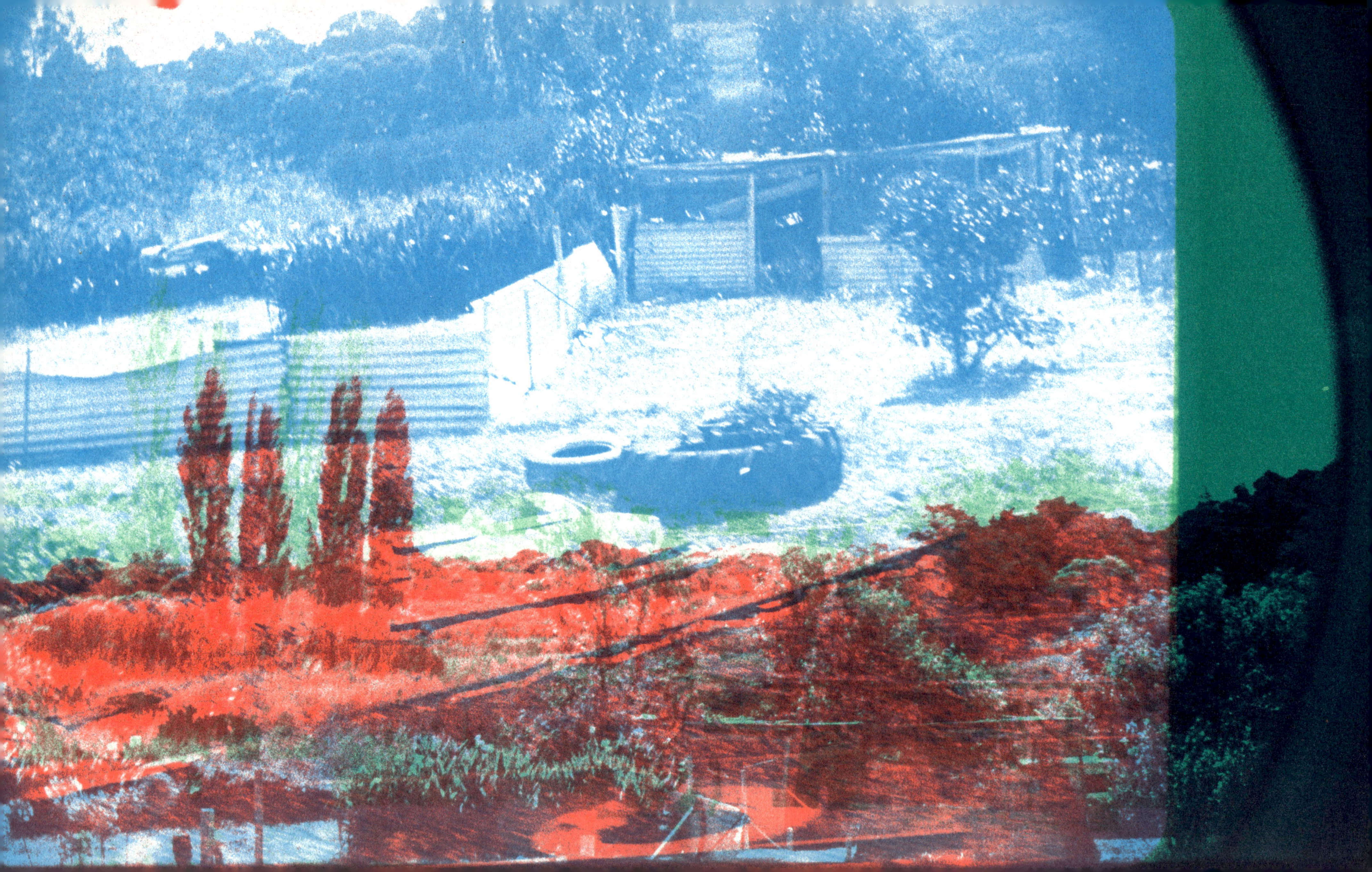

We have both shown *Zabriskie Point* to students extensively as it truly pictures, as Deleuze put it, "the colours of the world", and "the possibility of creating them, and of renewing all our cerebral knowledge".[11] The film's script allows for a level of improvisation and as such gets a high difficulty score.

The actors respond to conditions that are established and move within the given parameters of the script, the film retaining the sense the action emerged from one moment to the next, from one decision to the next. The anxiety and uncertainty of 1970 is reflected in the film, a time when everything was in a process of caving in, further and bizarrely corrupting our gestures. It has a strong sense of agency to it, a thread that runs through the whole film, which is in essence a story of two runaways (one escaping the law after a student riot, and the other from the betrayal of her bourgeois family). It pictures spontaneous volition and the electric energy of that in folk. The famous explosion scene at the end is part of this — the developer's mansion in the desert, built from the ill-gotten gains of property development — is blown up, seemingly as an act of telekinesis by the girl who looks at the developer's building cantilevered out from the craggy rock face and detonates it and all that it represents in her mind's eye, and we are pulled into that same swirling psychic space. It becomes, erupts into being, breaking down structures and blowing apart a rut.

11. Gilles Deleuze, *Cinema 2: The Time-Image*, trans. Hugh Tomlinson and Barbara Habberjam, Minneapolis: University of Minnesota Press, 1985, p. 205.

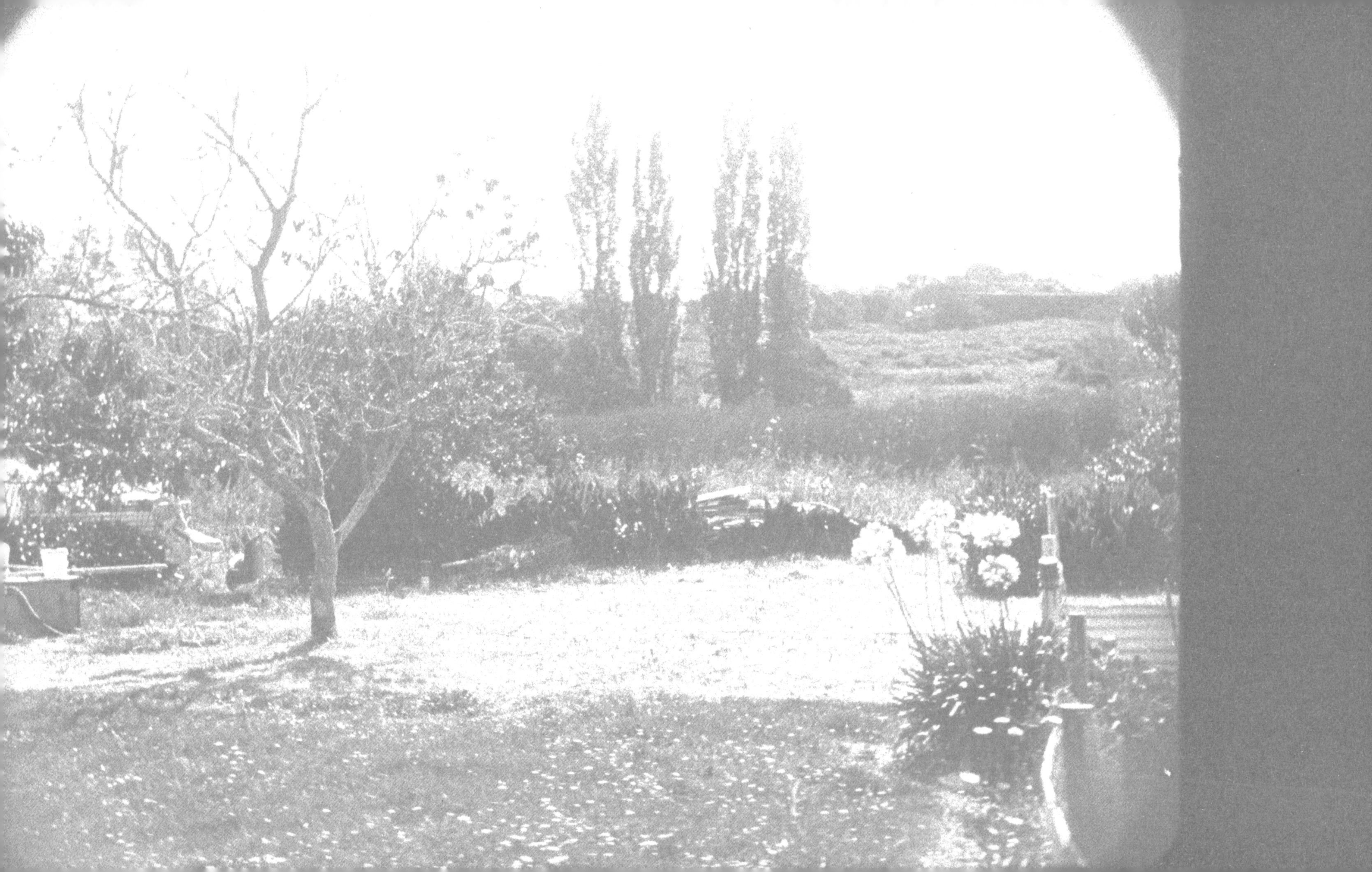

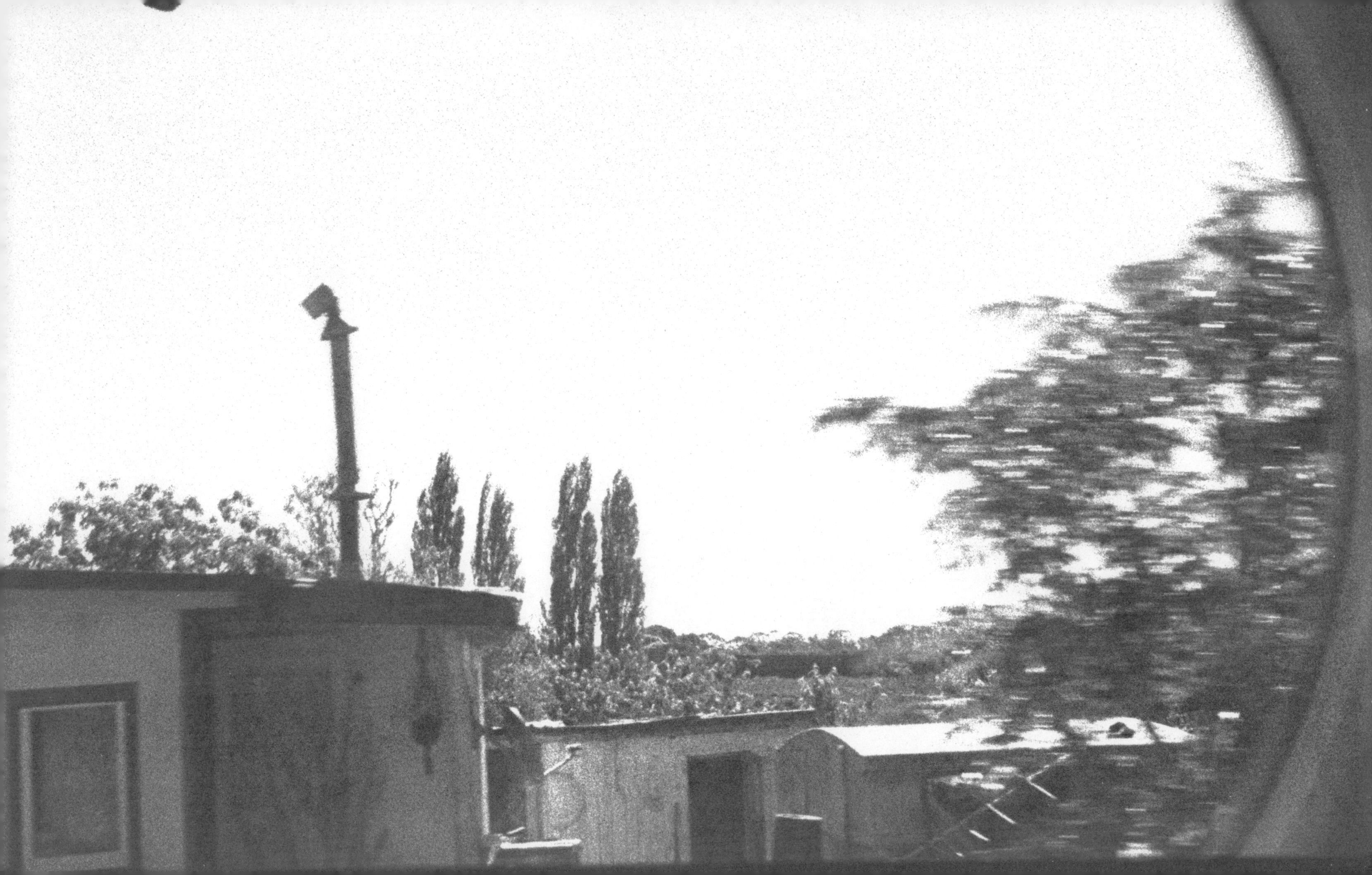

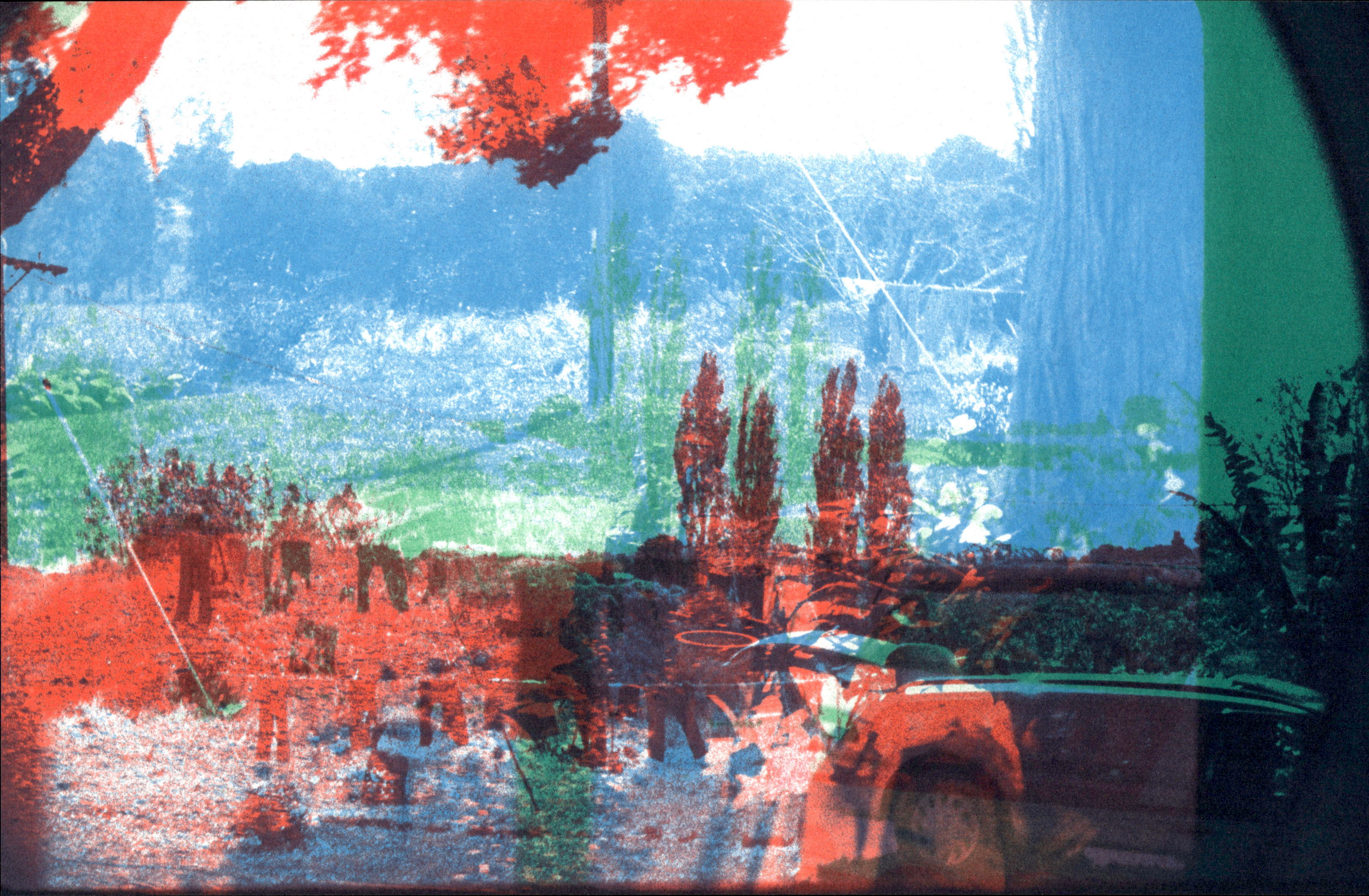

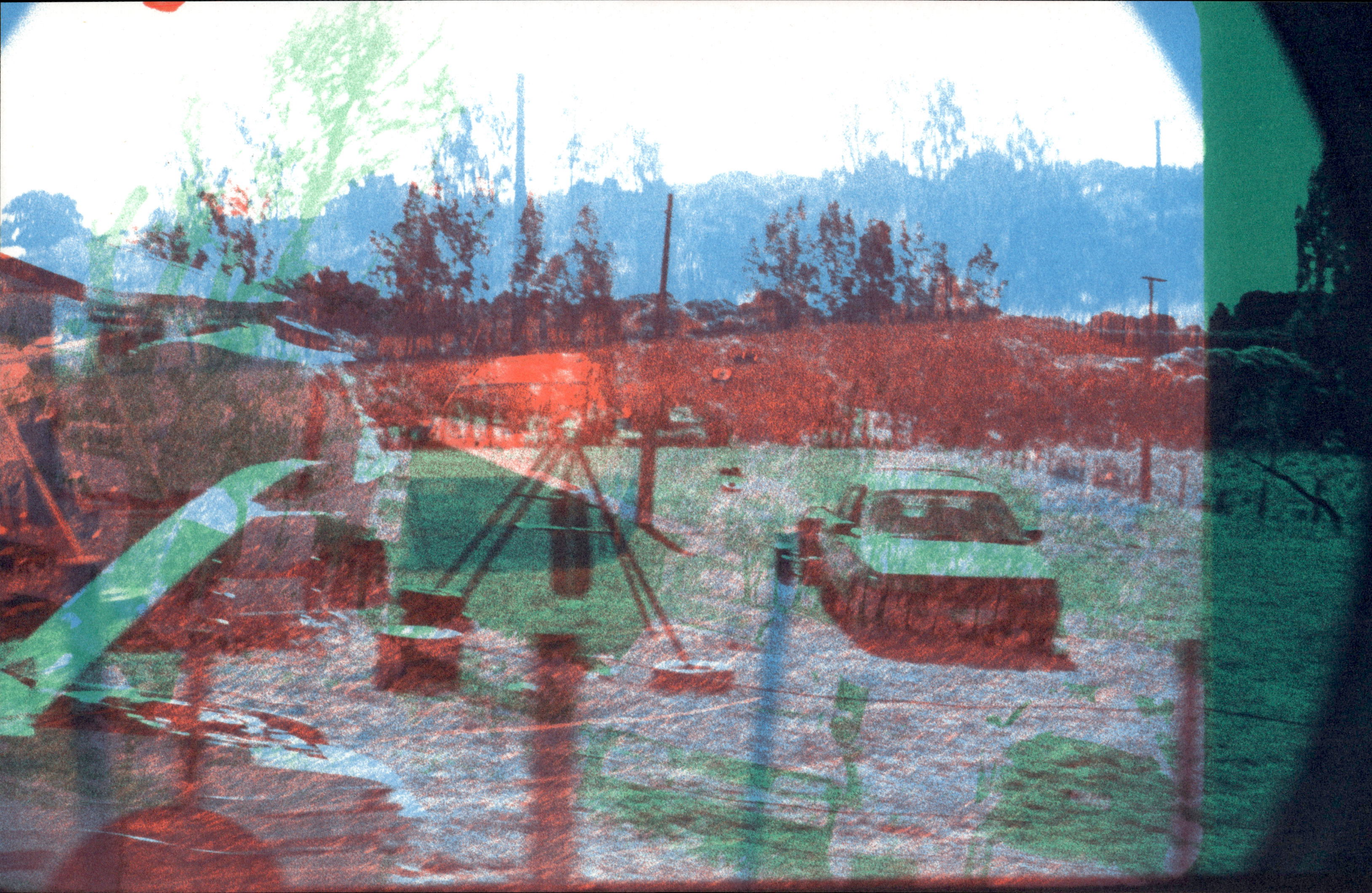

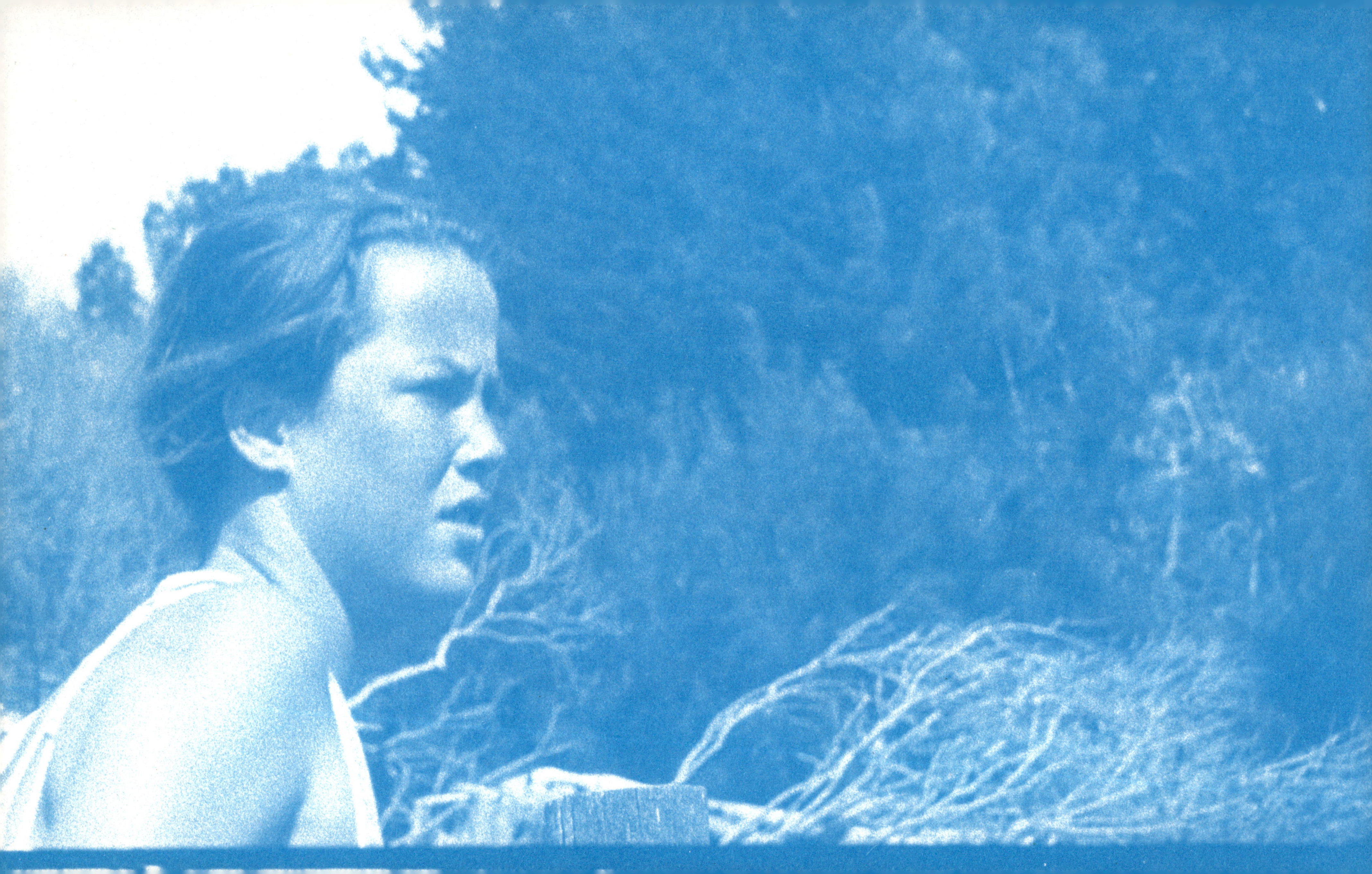

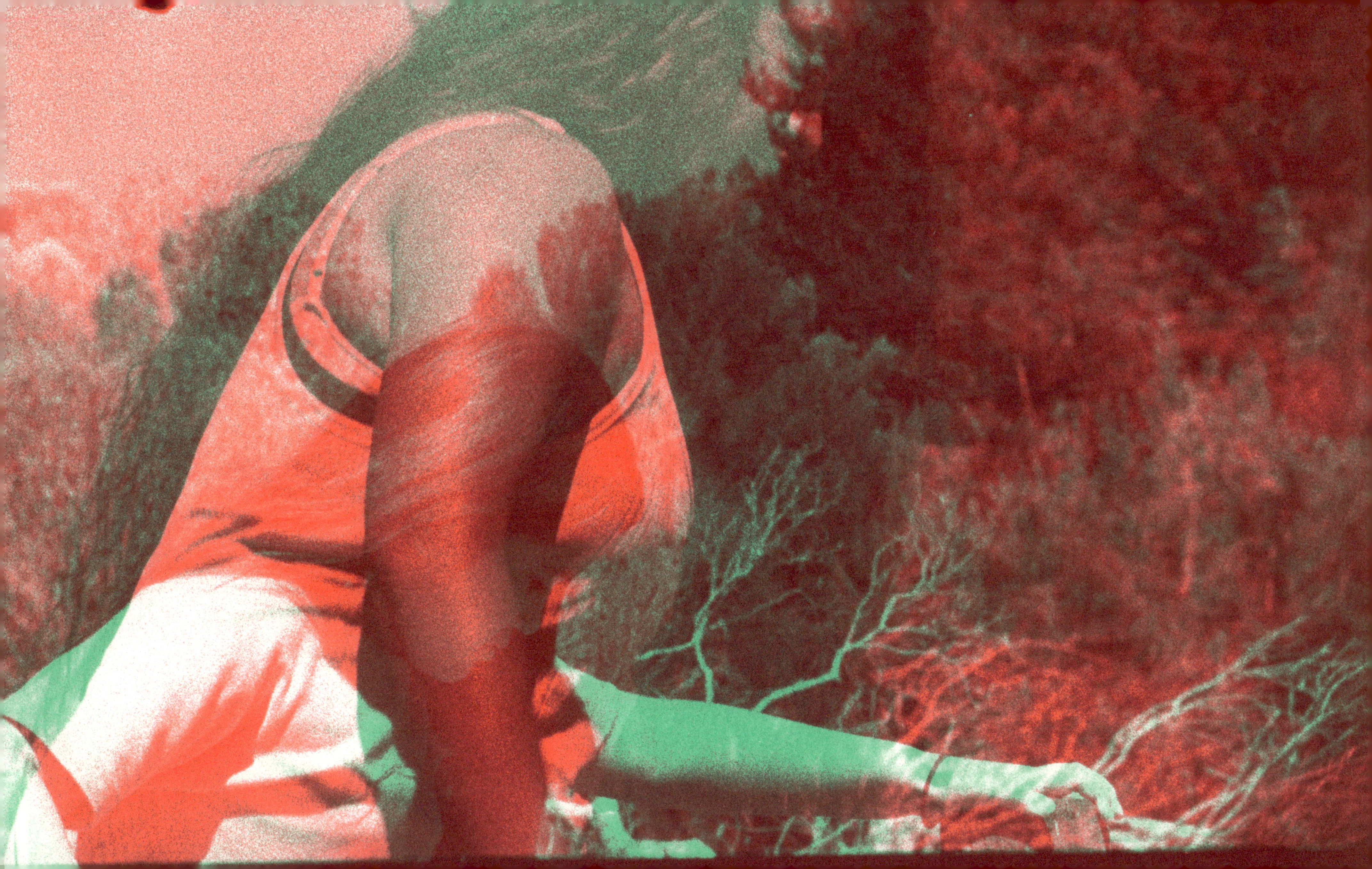

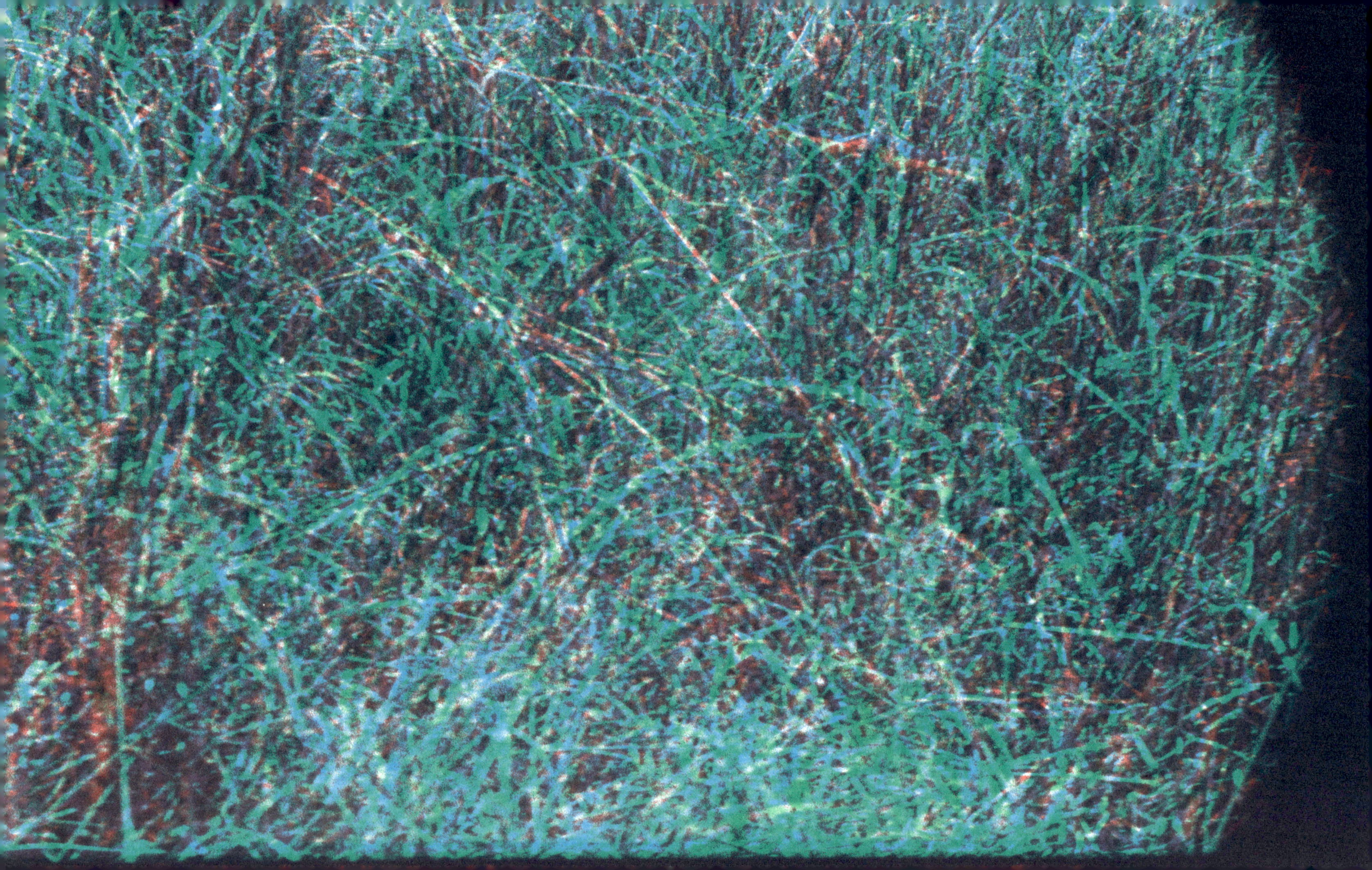

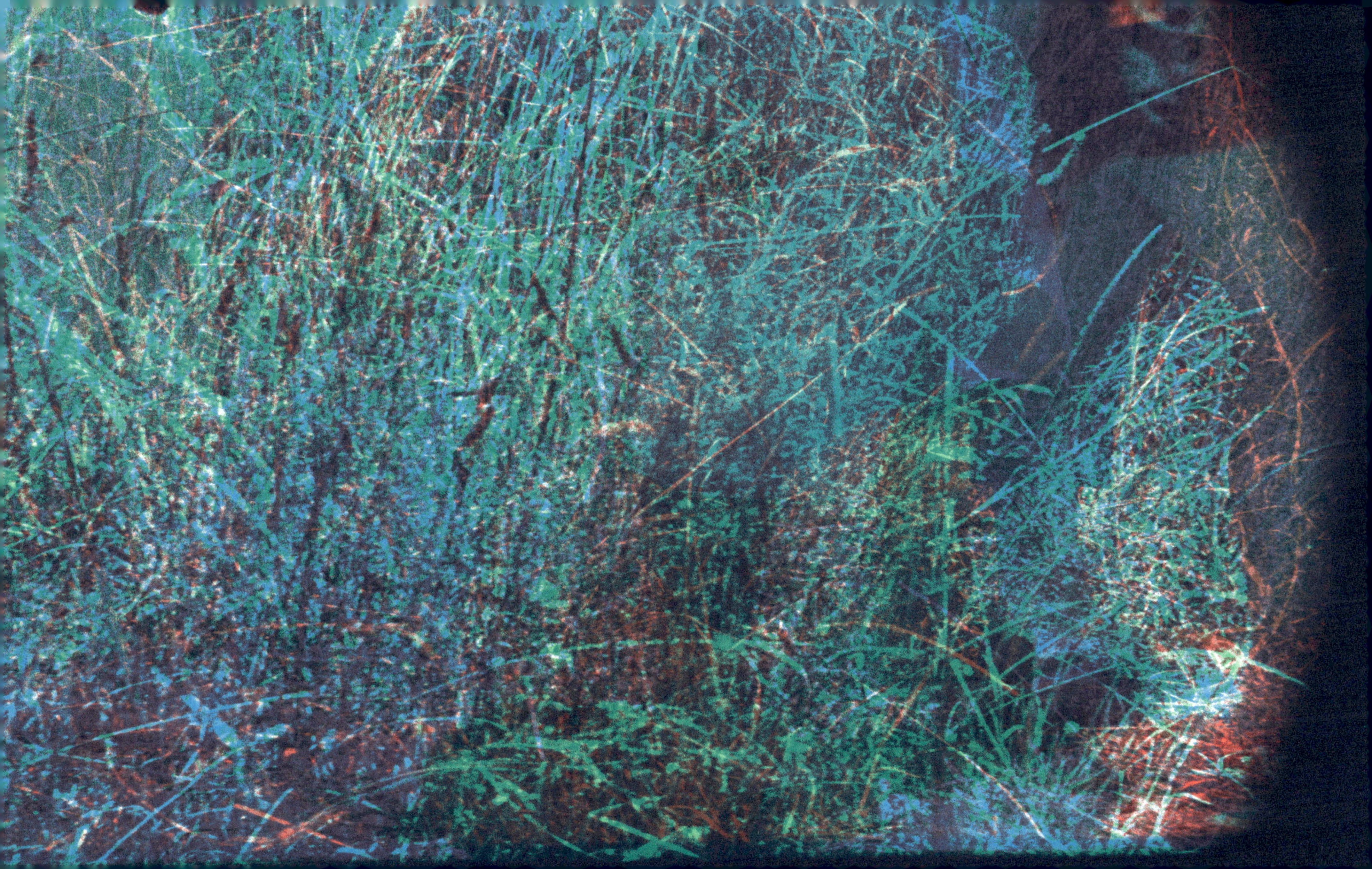

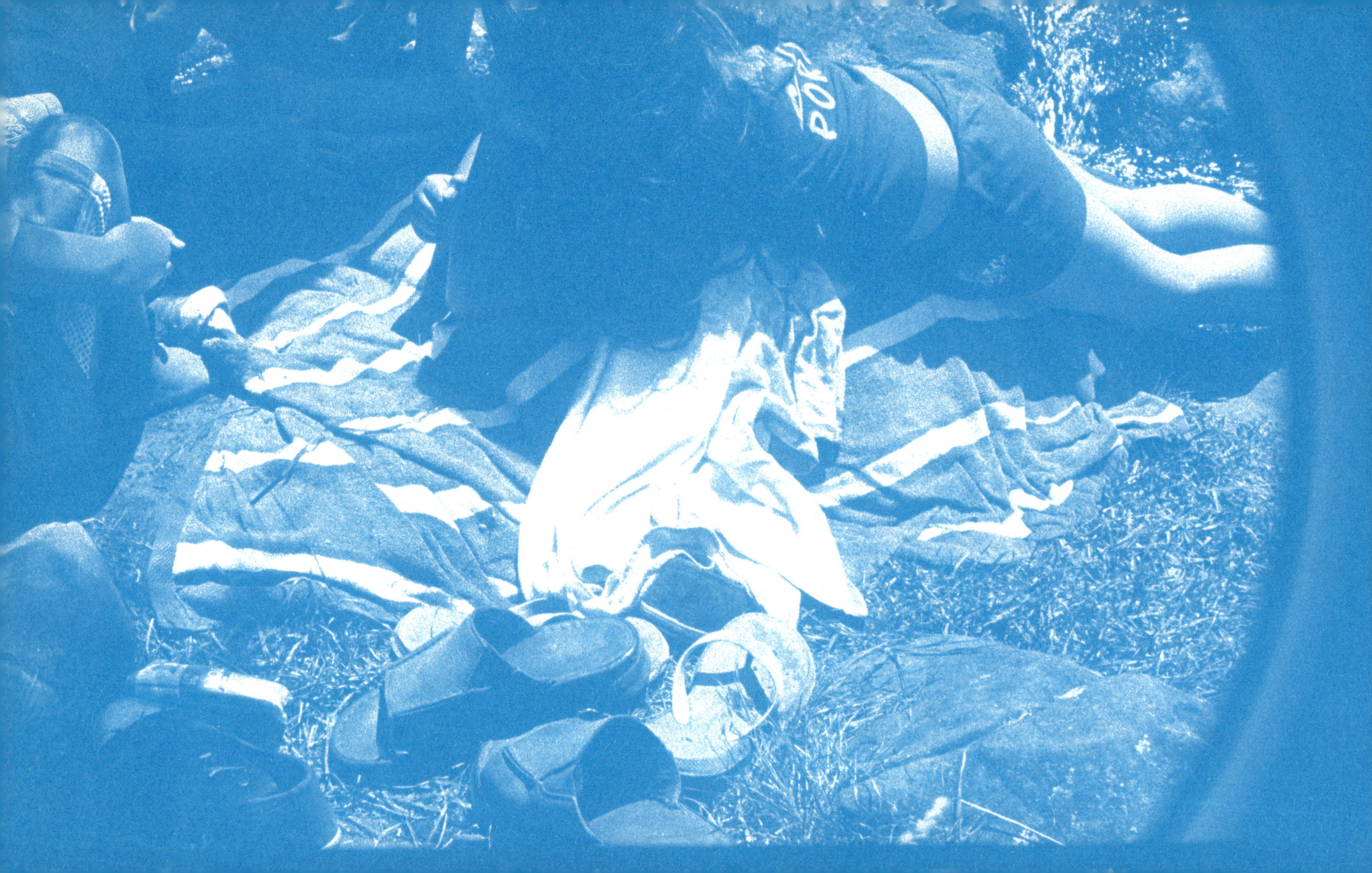

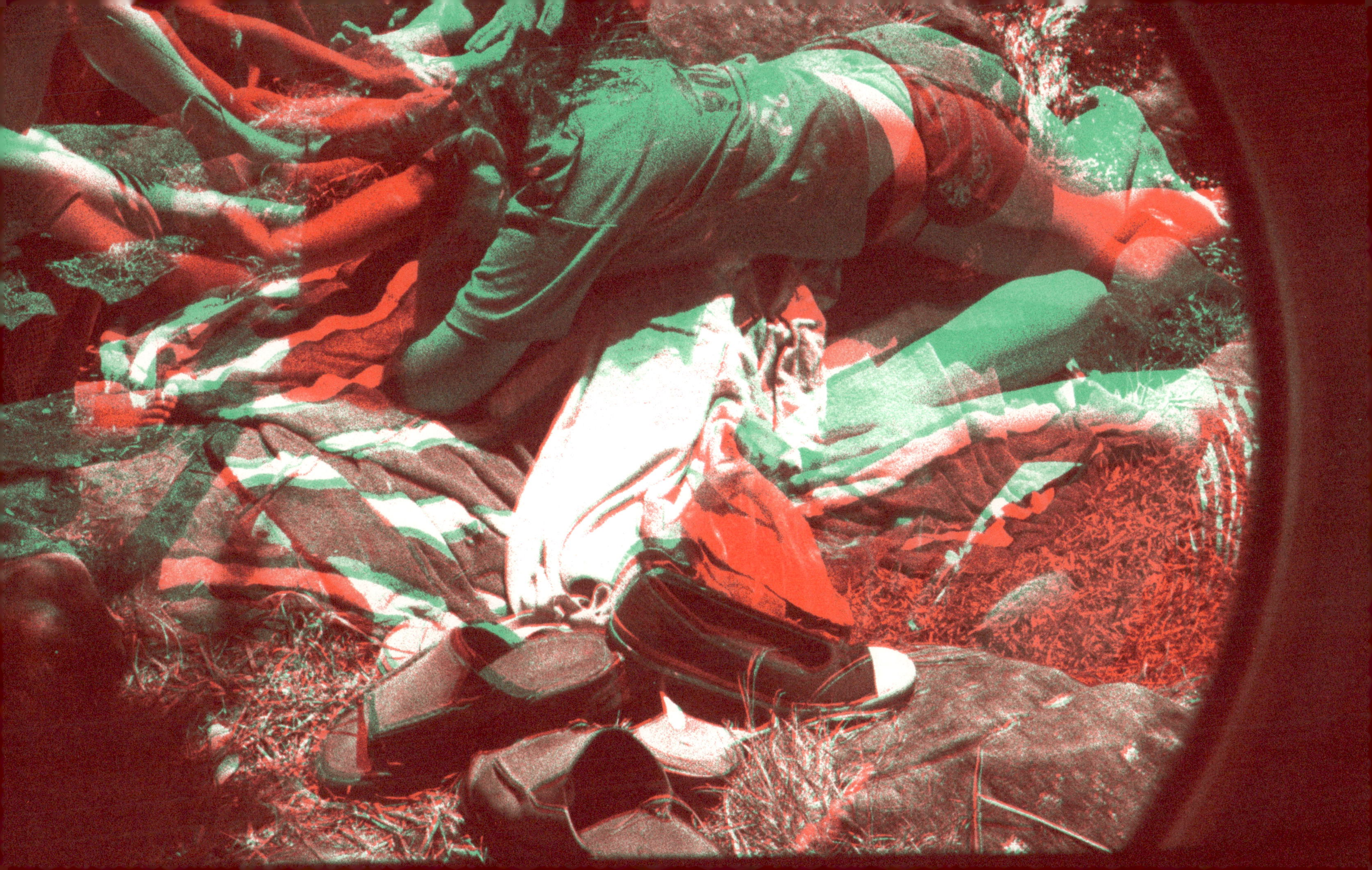

It's the slowness and the minutiae of this the explosion scene that is so enthralling. Using high-speed cameras and telephoto lenses the cinematography is florid and the screen blossoms with debris and objects gliding in space. The explosion replays over and over from different camera angles; a constant returning to an idea, a trauma, a fixation playing out outcomes and producing in Deleuzian terms, an any-space-whatever, the opening up of a space that is so abstract that is entirely time (time-image). We return to scenarios and repeat them: "all things themselves are dancing: they come and offer their hands and laugh and flee — and come back." It is a (literally) brilliant index of a thought process. If there is an immanence, it is a secular intensity, or a visionary, impassioned energy, a freedom borne out of love for freedom, a terrible commitment to self-determination unto death. Maybe this is what a god is, the vast interconnectedness of everything living, when we don't know how to act and are suspended in an any-space-whatever. Experimental films are often made of these abstract spaces — by presenting big blown out imagery as an abstract expressionist might have, a psychic space filling the screen.

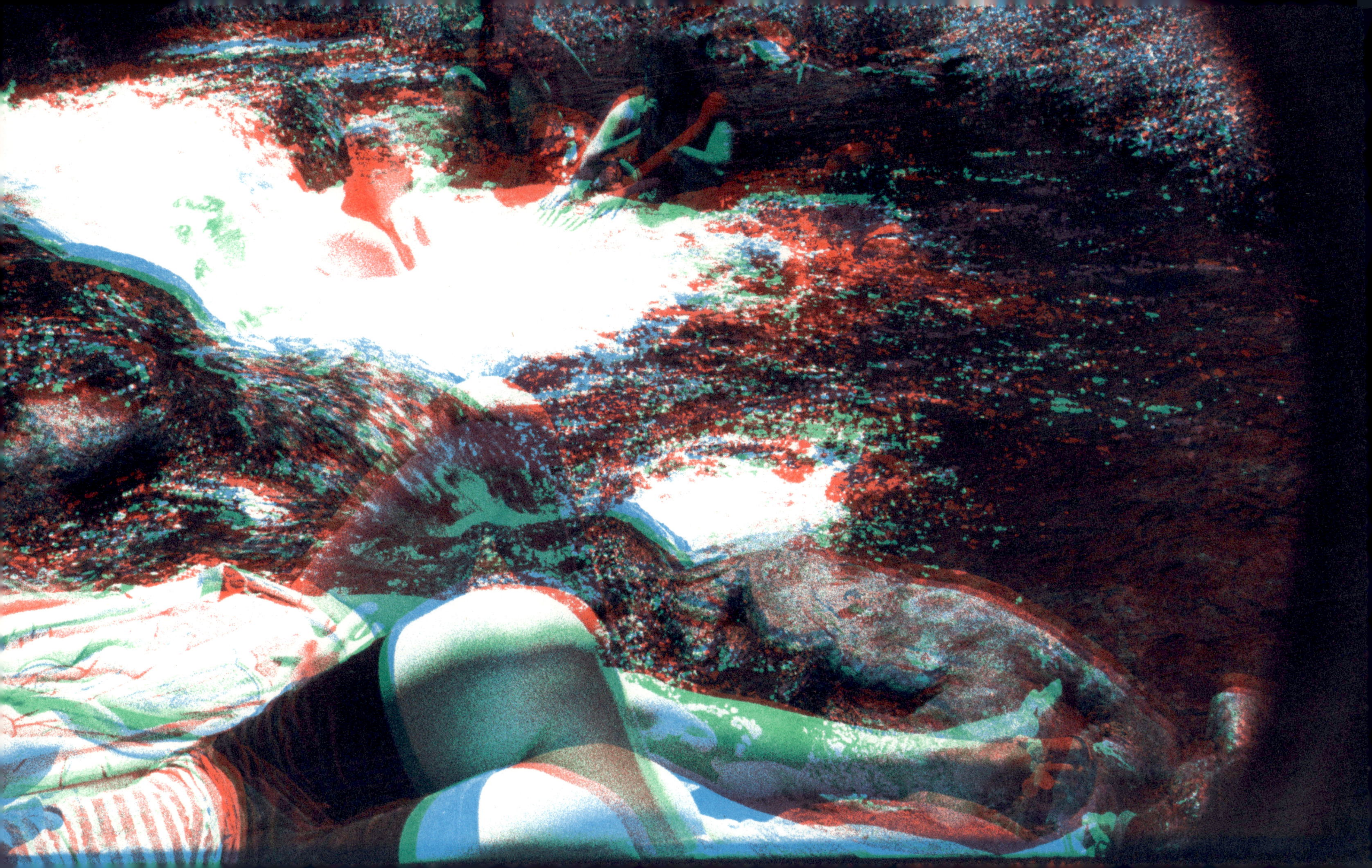

Once our place was covered in Kauri forest. The vast pillar-like trunks, however, made great masts for ships and long boards for the floors and walls of houses. Kauri makes a fragrant gum that when fossilised makes a beautiful amber that traps flecks of leaf matter and insects, the flotsam and jetsam of the forest. The commodification of this substance gave rise to a huge industry in the period following colonisation. Both Maori and Pakeha dug into the earth, making huge gaping holes in the body of the land to find this matter and laid it out in the sun which made it transparent and more saleable. The land too was divided and assigned titles. Water is harder to parcel, and entwined in this film is the relationship with the family river Wairua. Family connect to the river, the river as an ancestor. My family is the river and the self is surrendered to a greater flow. The film was named after a line from 'Tomorrow Never Knows', the last song on The Beatles' album *Revolver*: "Turn off your mind /Relax and float down stream / It is not dying / It is not dying / Lay down all thought / Surrender to the void / It is shining / It is shining / That you may see / The meaning of within / It is being / It is being…" We had both listened to this album a lot unbeknownst to each other as the film was being edited, one freely, the other under the insistence of a three-year-old in the back seat. Things that happen under roofs like this, ordinary things, are a kind of becoming. These are the whaka-iti Baxter spoke of in his *Jerusalem Daybook* (1970) — a making smaller, or making soft — that are the necessary condition for enlightenment. This film does not set up anything rational. It is blazed. There is no top to the head and energy is streaming out into space.

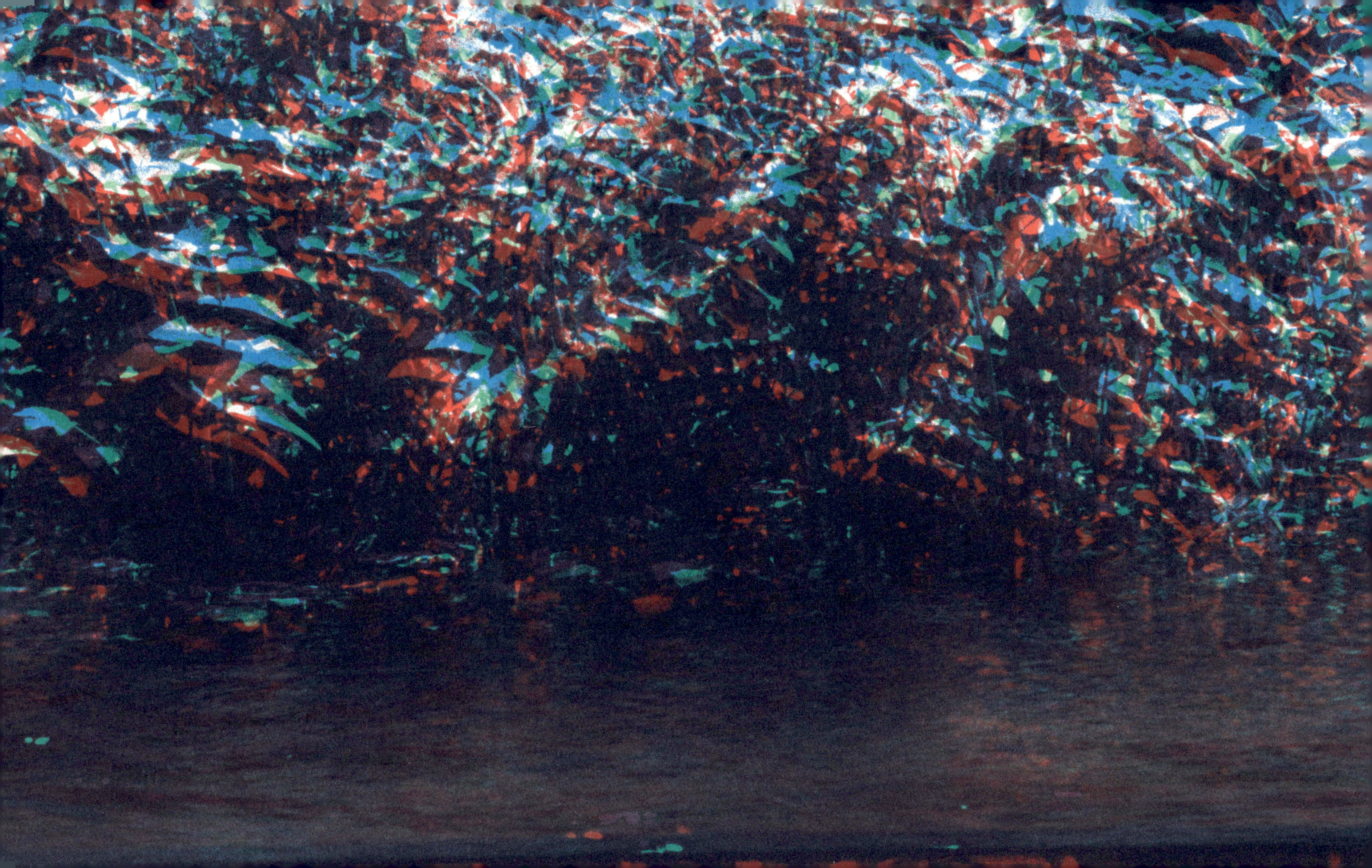

The supposed abstraction of the film dissolves as it becomes apparent that it is perhaps more realistic and reasonable than we may have first thought, using habitual thinking. Meditation is not a voiding of the mind but a practice of observation. This film can, in this sense, be seen as slowing down in order to see the way in which we are composed in layers. The way in which it sinks into direct apprehension of light and colour, of visual experience fused with emotional or human time (or into 'affect' as a psychoanalytic or philosophical theorist might explain direct apprehension) is again part of its ethical dimension: "Political resistance is constructed by an 'artisan' or artist' who follows this matter-flow in such a way as to turn it expressive, by rendering the singularities of the flow — before they have congealed into recognizable and representable forms — in affect. In this way the affect becomes a trajectory of transformation, inasmuch as the artist constructs from the continuous variation of matter an expression (affect) capable of embodying its continuous development, capable, that is, of producing a difference. The production of the new is therefore a fundamentally aesthetic and material process, involving the construction of sensible aggregates that are themselves creative."[12] And the karanga hangs in the air, for "Art has this strange prophetic function: it is made in the present, from the materials at hand, but calls out to something else."[13]

12. Simon O'Sullivan and Stephen Zepke, *Deleuze, Guattari and the Production of the New*, London: Routledge, 2008, pp.2–3.
13. Simon O'Sullivan. "The Production of the New and the Care of the Self" in O'Sullivan and Zepke, p.98.

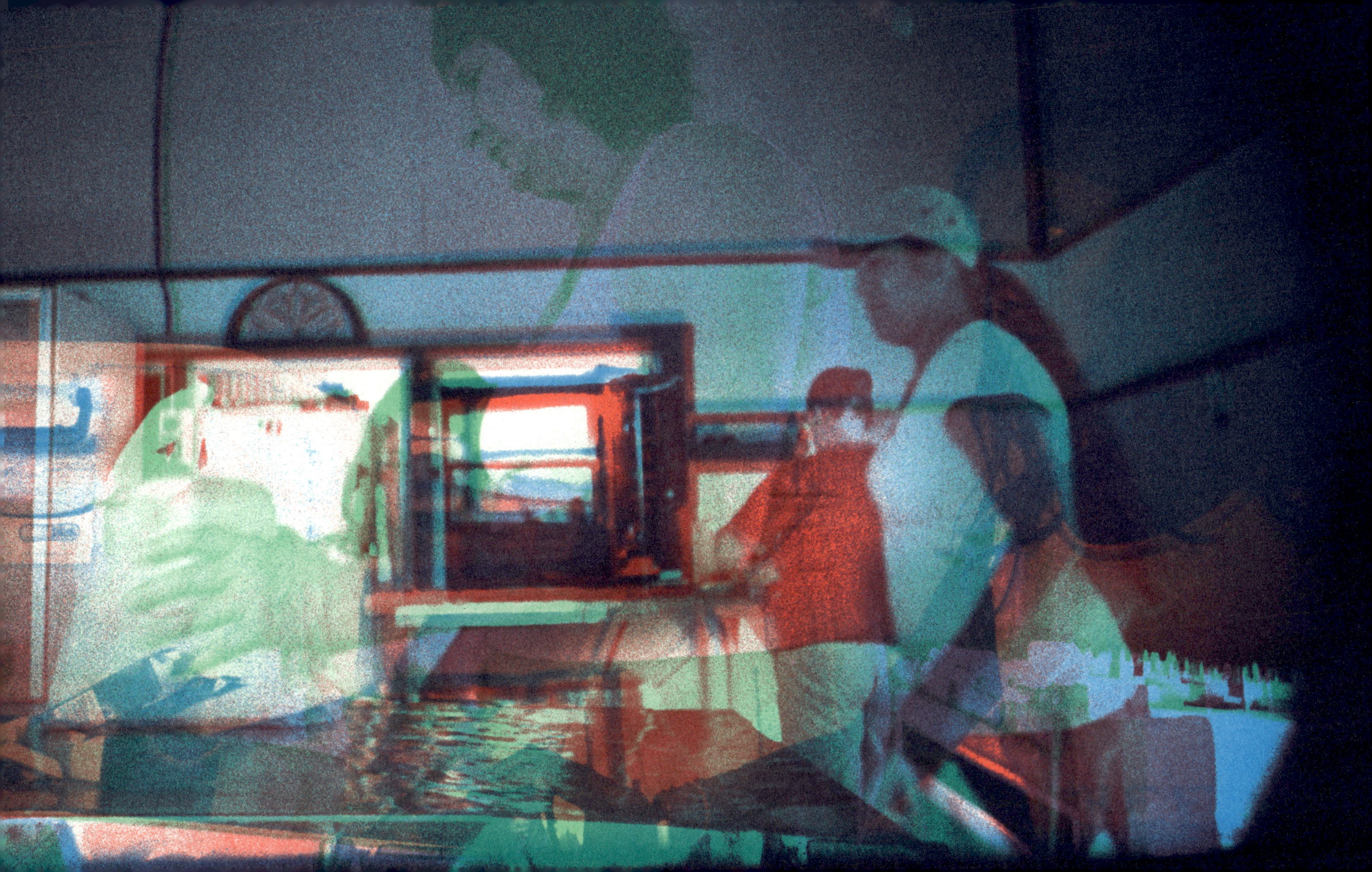

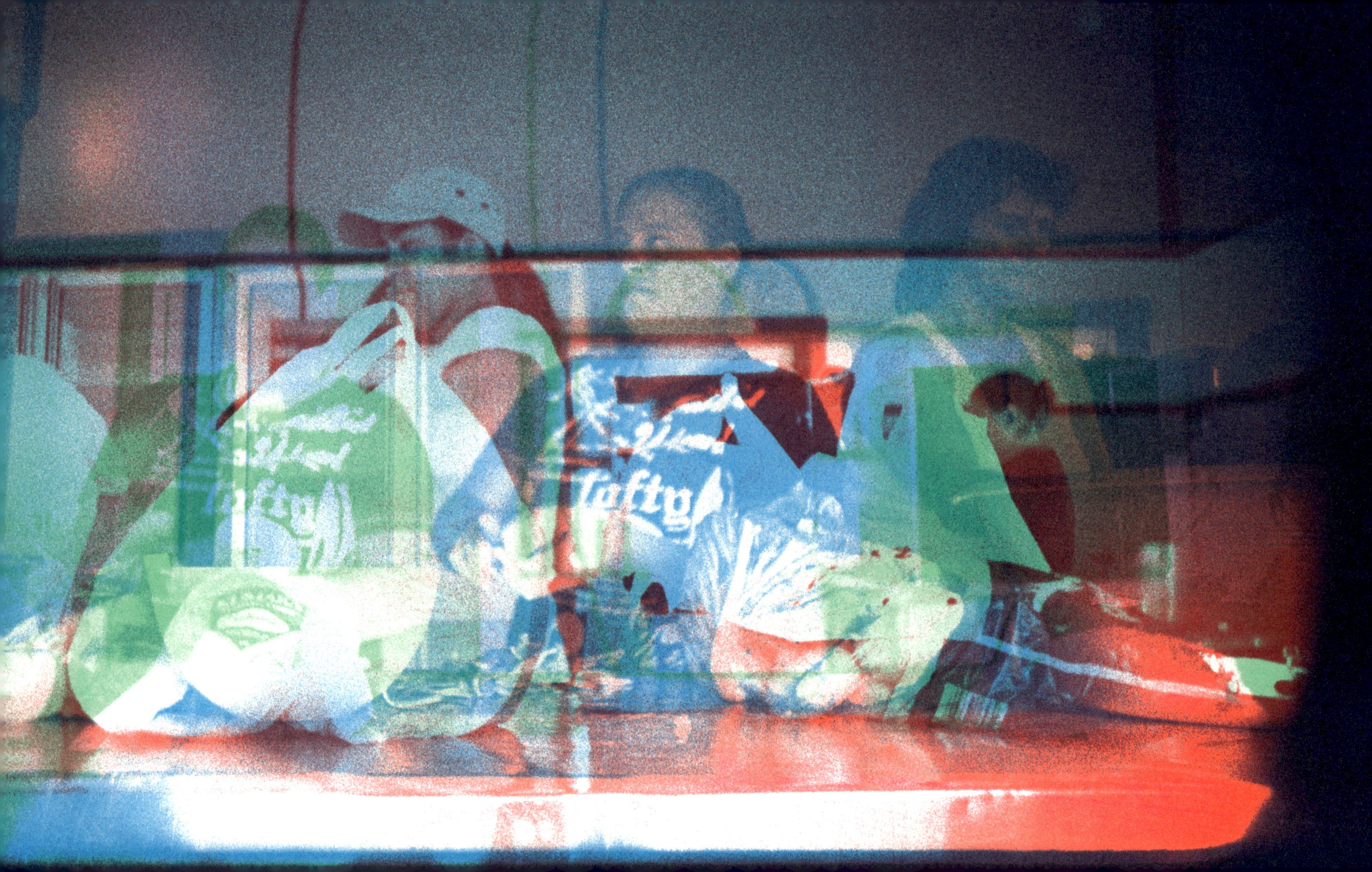

Nicolas Philibert's documentary *Every Little Thing* (1997) is set in the grounds of La Borde, the psychiatric hospital that Félix Guattari worked in for many years. Here, people were supported to evolve in their own ways, not given standards to adhere to. Nor was there any hierarchy of staff over patient — everyone pitched in contributing to the running of the place. In the film, the passing of time is measured through long takes of the tall Poplars that mark the surrounding grounds or by following residents walking around the borders of Le Borde. The trees moving in the wind and the people moving across the grass create a space or gap for reflection or introspection ("a certain stillness as the condition of genuine creativity"[14]). The very shape of the film houses the meaning of asylum being a place of care and shelter. It's not about rehabilitation, it's about acceptance and self-determinancy — everyone's already OK. Each year the residents of Le Borde annually perform a play, that is, all according to his or her willingness to participate. This time it is an absurdist piece *Operetta* by the Polish playwright Witold Gombrowicz, a complex theatre work that erupts into nonsense and joyful frivolity, the essence of which is captured in one of the choruses: "When human affairs can't be crammed into words, language explodes." The plays take place under the huge trees every summer against the backdrop of hundreds of thousands of buzzing leaves (like ambient black metal, a trope for synaptic feeling). People whom might be assumed to be catatonic, or mute, or lost in a puzzle of thought or meaning, blossom with the opportunity to engage in an avant-garde acceleration of sense, to take flight. Here those that have been the lightning rods for capitalist schizophrenia and the tortured family enact "an absolutely schizophrenic capital that releases self-organizing units of 'surplus value'"[15].

14. Ibid, p.7.

15. Ibid, p.8.

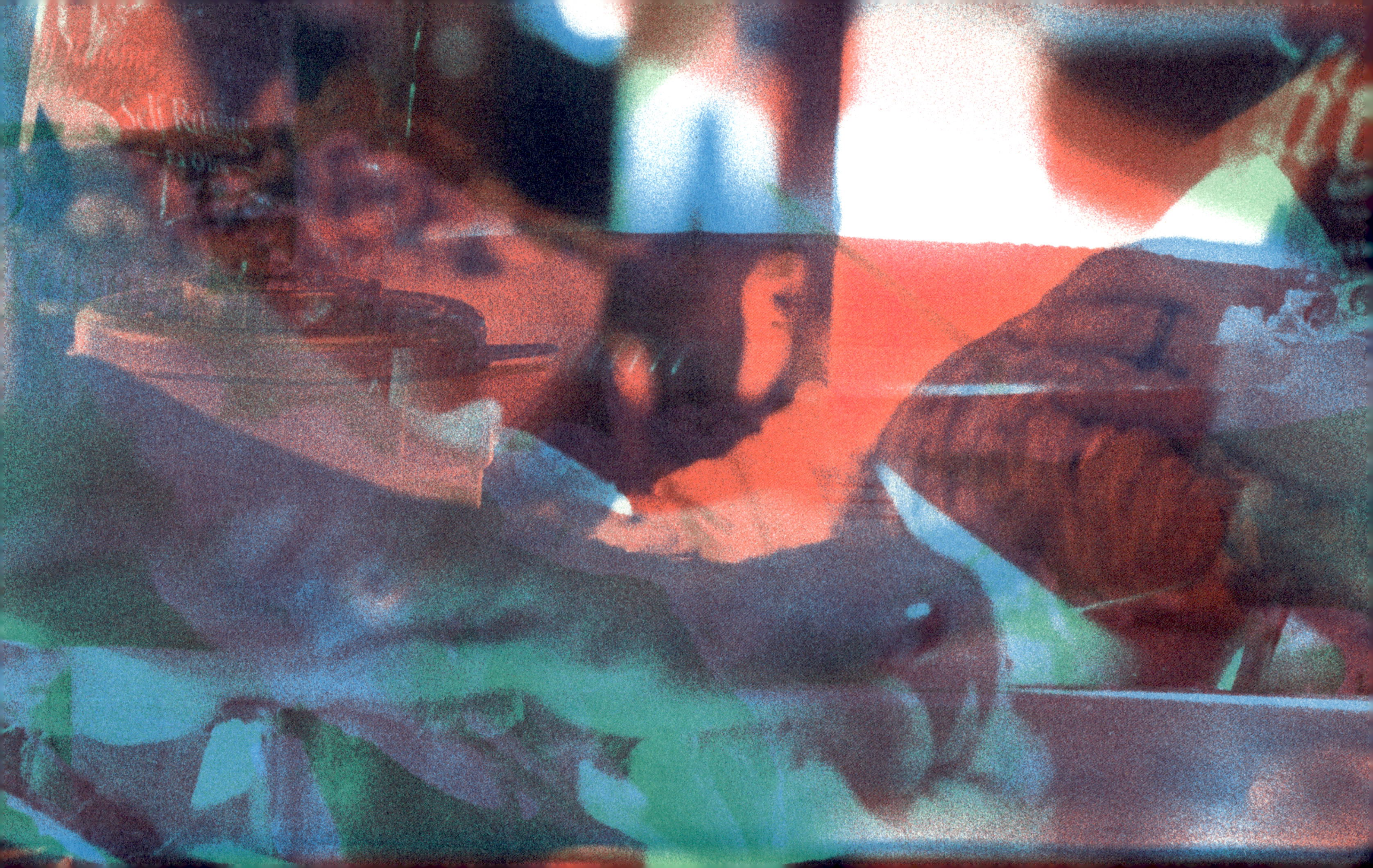

The film gently observed the gestures of people recreating themselves, their theatre an analogue for the transformation they dare to hope for. This huge house and its forest seem to reverse the action of traditional psychiatry-by-force, because "the more gestures lose their ease under the action of invisible powers, the more life becomes indecipherable".[16] All the time, the huge trees that dwarf the architecture are growing and moving through a cycle. Still verdant, the green has darkened a shade as they are about to turn. Their thousands of shimmering leaves mesmerise with how they look and sound at once, and they remind me of wiri, the trembling hand gestures of women performing waiata-ringa (literally "song of hands or arms"). These movements are talked of sometimes as figuring the interface between the mind and the body, the shimmering of water in the sun, heatwaves rising from the ground, and wind in the leaves.

16. Agamben, p.52.

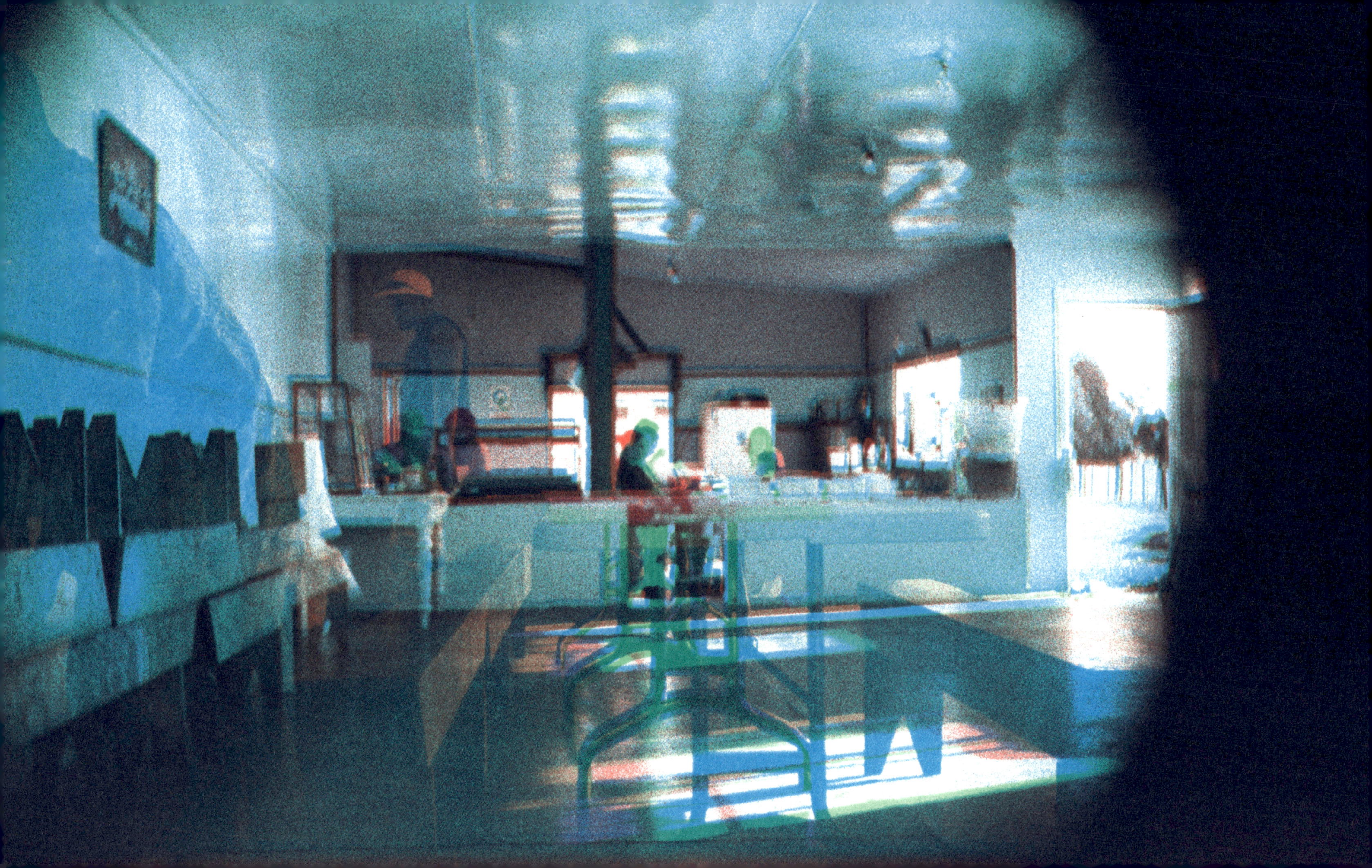

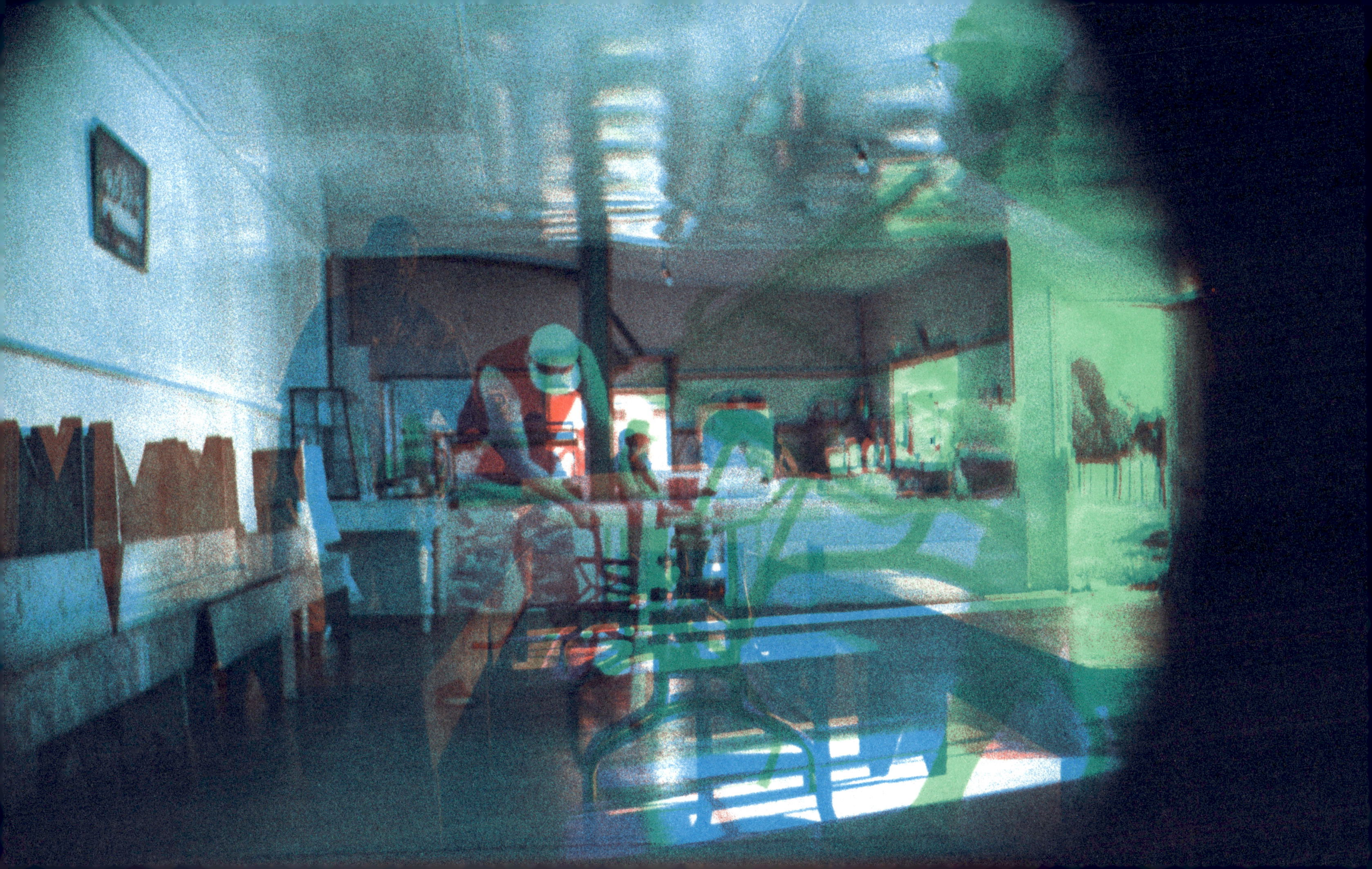

There is a layer in the leaf stem where it meets the twig that cuts the life off from the leaf, making it change colour and fall. I discovered this last winter when I could see a twig in the giant pin oak that had snapped and had held its brown leaves all winter hanging there like a gibbet. So, a tree is no different from us in that it has to let go on purpose. People seem to like to visit me here and say they feel safe and sit on my couch in a greenish light refracted off the foliage. Trees hold great force and it is no wonder that there are a percentage of men that cannot live with large trees on their property and they either refuse to live there or set about cutting them down, muttering about proliferation. It is no mistake that runes are made of fruitwood between flower and the setting of fruit. Why should not a tree tell us of the future? Here, all the native trees are evergreens with small noiseless leaves and do not show their skeletons in the winter.

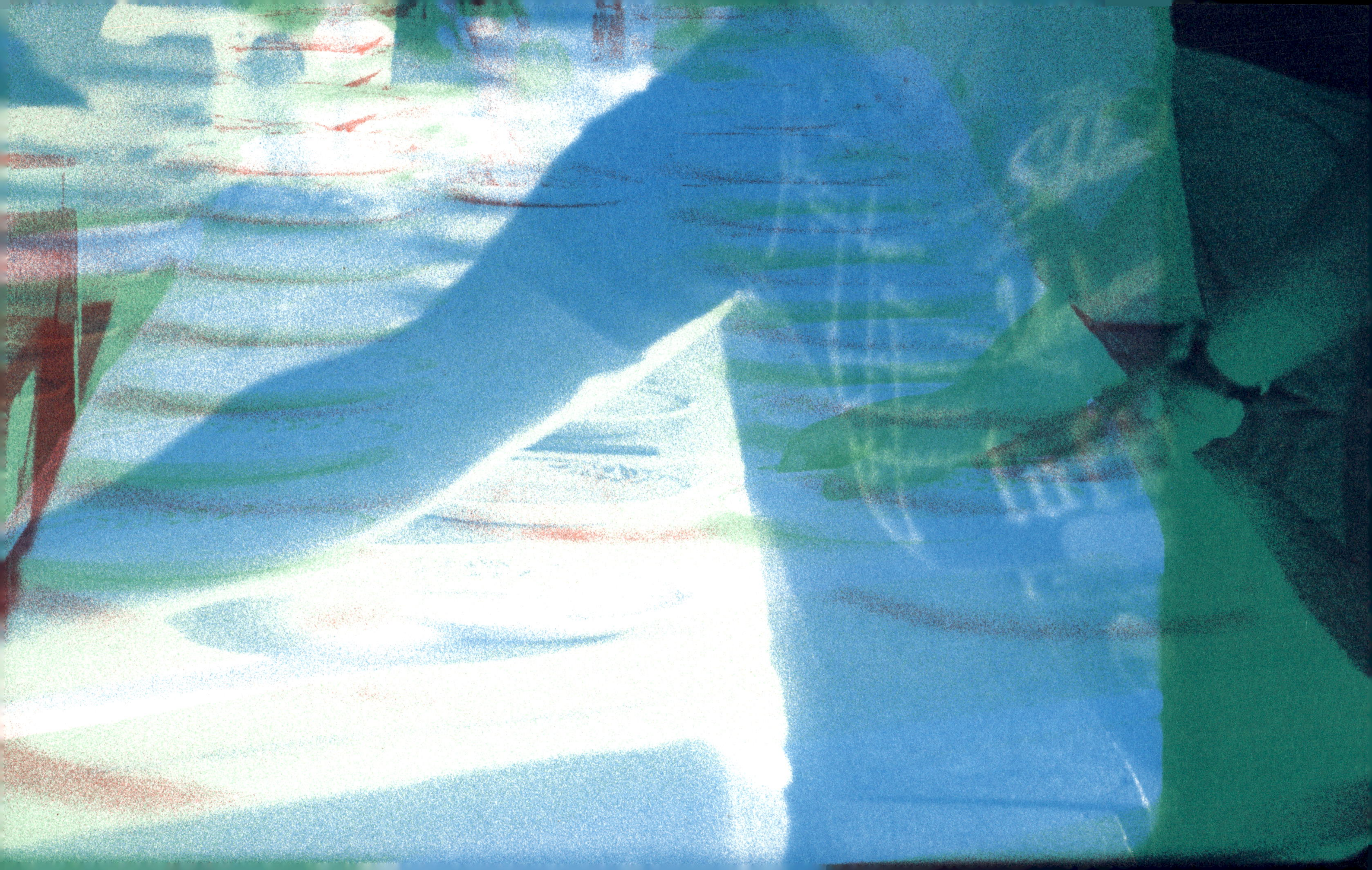

I am looking forward to the leaves being shed (not stripped) so I can see the edges of the trees, the crowd of tips of branch subsidiaries fanning out, the whole organism barely containing its energy. That it seems like an analogue for my own body — its capillary system supposedly making, feeding my edges, and me bursting beyond this supposed limit of the self into communal space — is something that Rainer Maria Rilke treated in *The Notebooks of Malte Laurids Brigge* (1910): "But outside, everything is immeasurable.

And when the level rises outside, it also rises in you, not the vessels that are partially controlled by you, or in the phlegm of your most unimpressionable organs: but it grows in the capillary veins, drawn upward into the furthermost branches of your infinitely ramified existence. This is where it rises, where it overflows from you, higher than respiration and, as a final resort, you take refuge, as thought on the top of your breath. Ah! Where next? Your heart banishes you from yourself, your heart pursues you, and you are almost already beside yourself, and you can't stand it any longer. Like a beetle that has been stepped on, you flow from yourself, and your lack of hardness or elasticity means nothing anymore."

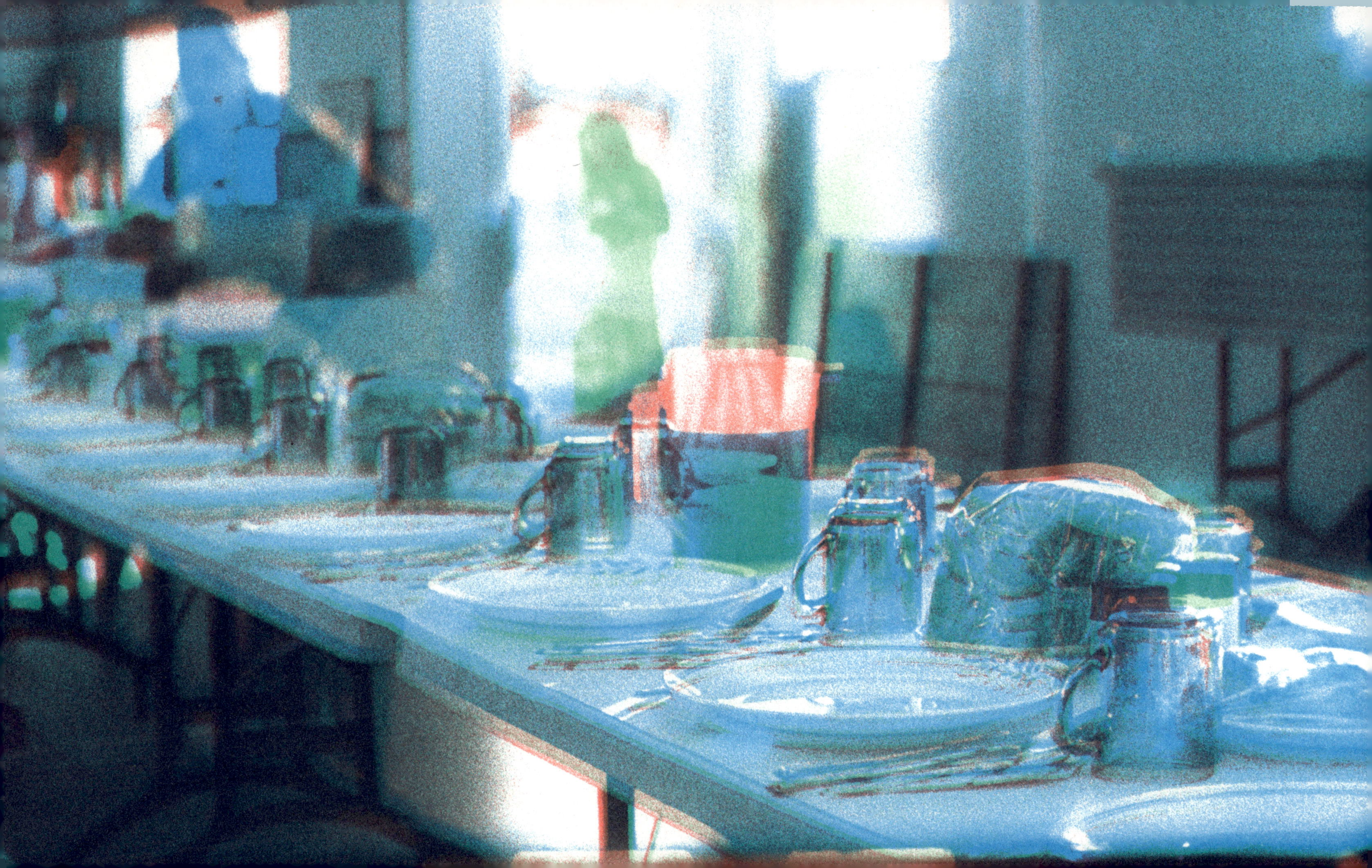

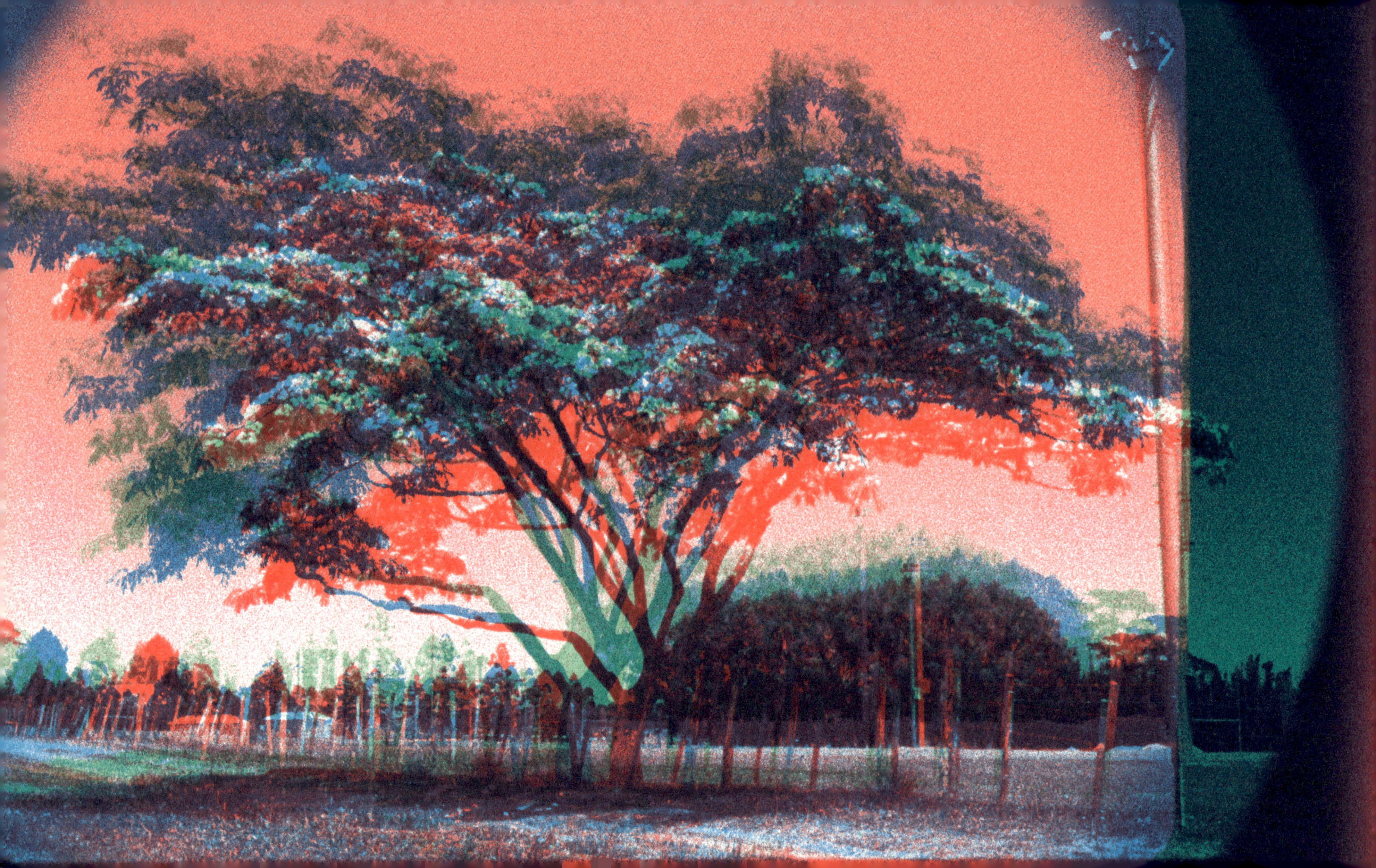

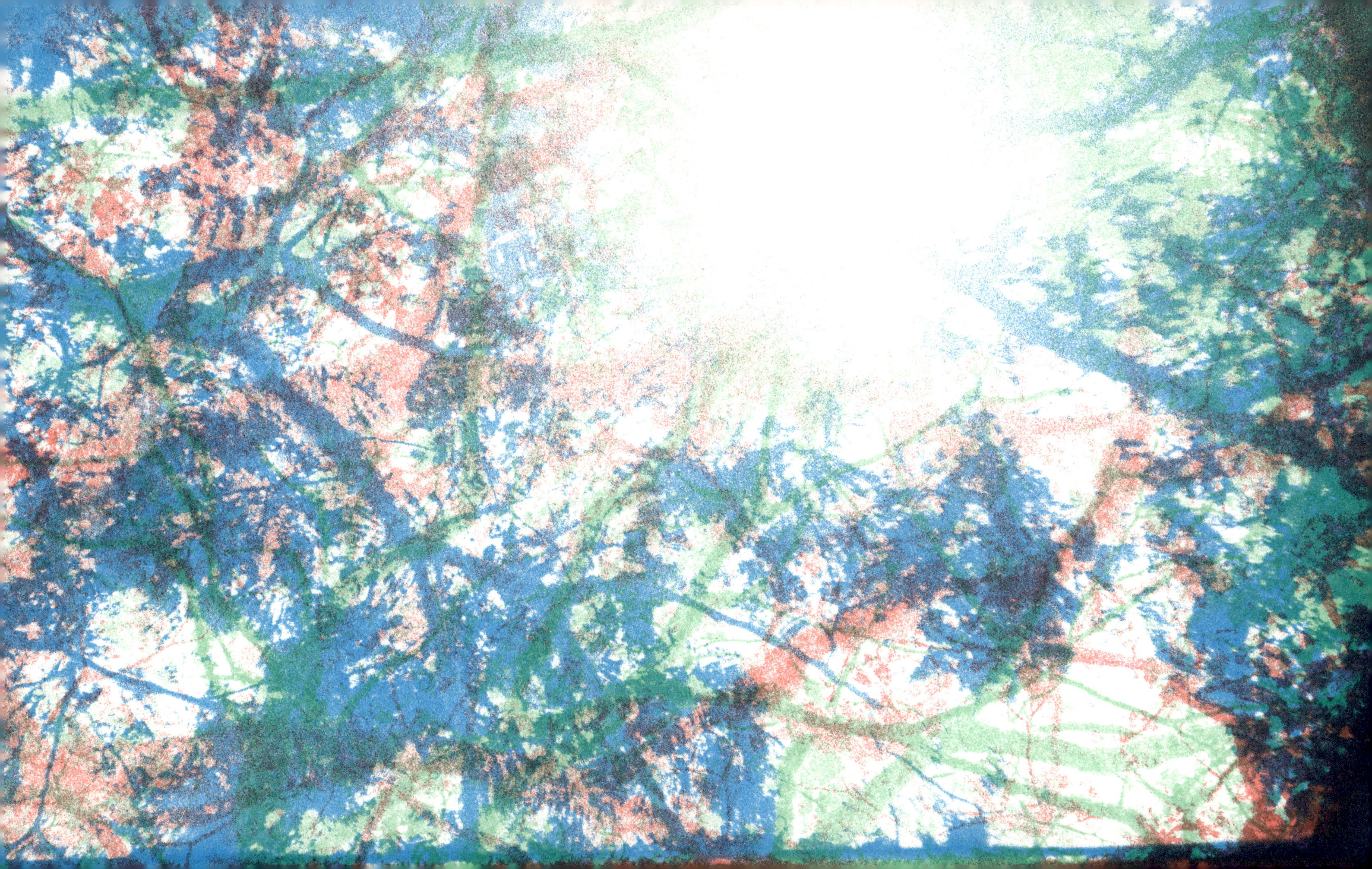

On the wall of the kitchen is a poster that is headed up "virtues — the gifts of character / He whakamaoritanga na Tawai Hauraki-Te rangi. He taonga aroha mo nga mokopuna mo apopo". An array of different positive attributes of self are listed and summarised in spiral form with 'assertiveness' in the middle. It seems to say that people ought not open their mouth until they have the other myriad of virtues down. Or is it that we must start with utterances but be aware that what we articulate may split into a spectrum of colours, our intent to work together functioning as a prism? Oral traditions often prefer to continue to pass on information carefully and purposefully rather than publish for this very reason. Sovereignty is sometimes best practised discretely as self-possession is hard to learn in the first place (if you don't know it already) and to hang onto in the second. I've heard it takes at least hundred years for a community to be able to process something that went wrong before right action can be taken, reminding me to accept that this sort of slowness and complexity is not just OK, but the root of something huge and multi-coloured.